A UNICORN

IN A WORLD OF DONKEYS

MIA MICHAELS

A UNICORN

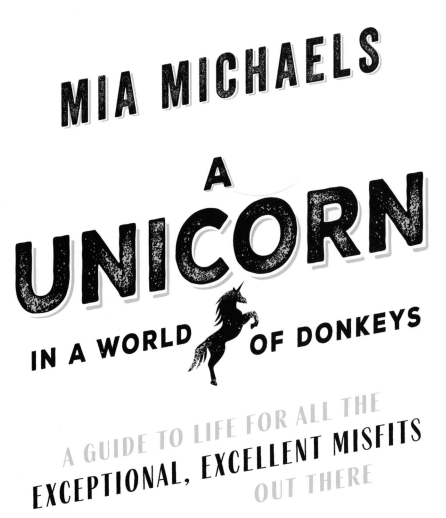

IN A WORLD OF DONKEYS

A GUIDE TO LIFE FOR ALL THE EXCEPTIONAL, EXCELLENT MISFITS OUT THERE

SEAL PRESS

The Hachette Speakers Bureau provides a wide range of authors for speaking events. To find out more, go to www.hachettespeakersbureau.com or call (866) 376-6591.

Seal Press
Hachette Book Group
1290 Avenue of the Americas, New York, NY 10104
sealpress.com
@SealPress

First Edition: May 2018

Printed in the United States of America

Published by Seal Press, an imprint of Perseus Books, LLC, a subsidiary of Hachette Book Group, Inc.

The Seal Press name and logo is a trademark of the Hachette Book Group.

The publisher is not responsible for websites (or their content) that are not owned by the publisher.

Print book interior design by Chrissy Kurpeski
Typeset in Andrade Pro

Library of Congress Cataloging-in-Publication Data has been applied for.

ISBNs: 978-1-58005-772-1 (hardcover), 978-1-58005-775-2 (ebook)

LSC-C

10 9 8 7 6 5 4 3 2 1

To my beautiful Mom and Dad up in Unicorn heaven

*To my fearless and extraordinary big sis, Dana—
you inspire me more than you will ever know*

And to Lily Pop Michaels

CONTENTS

I AM MIA

THE WORLD WORSHIPS THE ORIGINAL.

Unicorns are the originals of the universe.

I am one of them.

Nothing about my life has been "normal." It's certainly not "normal" to have had model parents—and, by *model,* I definitely don't mean "perfect." My parents were actual models, beautiful hippies from the 1960s. My father, Joe Michaels, was the original square-jawed, flinty-eyed Marlboro Man with a mustache, a cowboy hat, a horse, and, of course, the cigarette. My mom, Ruth Johnson, was one of the Bunnies at the original Playboy Club in Miami Beach. She had sexy Swedish curves and platinum blonde hair that fell all the way down to her cottontail. The Marlboro Man and the Playboy Bunny met at a nightclub in Manhattan one random night, and didn't leave each other's side for the next fifty years, which isn't so normal either these days.

After fleeing the predatory world of modeling in New York, my parents left the city behind and followed the sun all the way down to Coconut Grove, Florida, to find whatever work they could, which, ironically, turned out to be more modeling. My sister, Dana, was born first, followed by me three and a half years later. At the time, my parents lived on a houseboat called *The Meatball* (they had meatballs in common, culturally: Dad's family was

Italian and Mom's was Swedish). My nickname from infancy was Bam Bam, like the *Flintstones* character, because of my supernatural strength. Mom told stories about seeing the furniture suddenly start moving, and then finding me in diapers behind it, pushing my little heart out with one hand while sucking my thumb with the other.

The Meatball wasn't much more than a floating shack, and even my antiestablishment parents didn't think it was a safe place to raise a young family after I threw myself in the bay from my high chair. Soon enough we moved to dry land, to a house that was, we would soon learn, haunted with ghosts and spirits. Most of the mysterious noises and moving or disappearing objects were in the living room. At night, you could hear the sound of glasses tinkling and people laughing, as if there was a perpetual, spectral cocktail party in there. Totally true story: when we moved out several years later, the new owner called my dad and said he'd been doing some renovations. Then he asked, "Did you know a steel pentagram was built into the roof?" Uh, no. Mom did a little research and we found out the house had been originally designed and constructed by a medical doctor who was known to be a practicing warlock. He regularly held parties and séances for his coven in the living room where we heard all those ghostly party noises. In this haunted house, I spent the formative years of my life.

So not normal.

In my very early years, I wore metal braces on my legs and special shoes on my feet—aka, the Forrest Gump kiss of death. I had an uncommon (but not unheard of) childhood limb growth discrepancy. My hip, leg, and feet bones weren't developing at the same rate, making one foot bigger, and my hips turned inward. Walking was difficult, and my movements were jerky and spastic. To go anywhere, just walking across the room or down the hallway at school, I had to fight for every inch of progress. Remember, this was in Florida, where wearing long, heavy pants to hide the braces wasn't a practical option.

My looks were always considered bizarre. I was taller and thicker than anyone in my class, including the boys. The other kids looked at me like I was an alien with my odd physical strength. I once picked a girl up and threw her into a wall for stealing my teddy bear. (She never touched my teddy bear again!) So, when the other kids called me a "retard" and "fatso" they did it from a safe distance.

Needless to say, I didn't have a lot of friends. I learned very early on that the strangest, most misunderstood, least apologetic person in the room is usually her own best company.

I LEARNED VERY EARLY ON THAT THE STRANGEST, MOST MISUNDERSTOOD, LEAST APOLOGETIC PERSON IN THE ROOM IS USUALLY HER OWN BEST COMPANY.

When my parents gave up modeling for good and supported their family by getting real jobs, they didn't get "normal" ones, like teacher or lawyer. Dad, who'd never danced professionally, decided to open a dance studio in our new house, and Mom sat at the front desk and managed the place. He'd always been a dance lover, taking Dana and me to New York City every year for a week of Broadway shows, dance performances, and ballets. I was rapturously entranced by the ballerinas and fantasized about becoming one, despite my physical problems and my unusual size.

I developed excellent technique from growing up in a dance studio my whole childhood. When I turned twelve, my well-meaning teachers at the after-school arts program thought I was too fat and rebellious to be a ballerina. They advised me of the only realistic options: (1) starve myself, or (2) quit ballet. I could have food or my dream, but not both.

At this point, the "normal" thing to do for a big-boned girl like me would have been to quit ballet in frustration and resentment, hate myself, and go crawl under a rock (a large one). I was a great dancer, I just didn't look like one. I couldn't let my dream die without a fight, though, so I tried starvation on and off for a solid week. Needless to say, severe calorie restriction didn't last. I love food way too much. In a fit of frustration with not losing weight and my disgust with required thinness, I stopped dieting *and* dancing in one fell swoop.

To fill the vacuum that quitting created, I hung out with the wrong crowd and did drugs. My wasted teenage years stand as the most self-destructive and confused time of my life. I lost my center, a sense of who I was, and spun wildly out of control, even dropping out of high school just a few weeks before graduation. My parents kept telling me that my life didn't make sense without dance because I had a calling, and they were right. With my options limited, I grudgingly put my leotards back on and started teaching classes at Dad's studio. Rediscovering my first love felt like a homecoming. I got myself back together, I went back to school and earned my GED and threw myself into a renewed life, with dance and creativity at its core.

The warrior was born. I realized I'd been fighting the same fight—to be 100 percent myself and focused on realizing *my* dreams—the whole time. Dana went to college and later medical school. That was right for her. For me, college would have been like pushing the PAUSE button on my life, while every impulse in my body and mind told me to punch PLAY. I didn't care what people were supposed to do, or what was typical, expected, or normal. I had a dream, and *no one*—including my darker self—was going to tell me to give up on it.

🦄

I've had plenty of ups and downs as I've galloped my way on what I call "the Rainbow Path" of creativity and outside-the-mainstream living and dreaming. Every time I was knocked down, I got back up and found that my Unicorn horn—the mark of being different, magical, unmatched—got a little longer and thicker. I don't feel like I've reached the stratosphere of creativity I'm aiming for—yet. I've been applauded by some for being "bold and innovative" and criticized in equal measure by others for being "difficult and too risky." Many times in the last thirty years of my professional life, I've wondered, "What the hell have I gotten myself into?" But in my heart, I always knew that the unconventional life was my only option, however terrifying it can be.

How could I be anything but strange? I was the weirdest kid in the room at five, and I'm still the oddest person to walk into the room at fifty. Most of my adult experiences, good and bad, relate back to my peculiar childhood and have contributed to making me an extraordinary human being. It took many years on a forever-steep learning curve to figure out how to be me unapologetically and to accept every bizarre part of my past. When I stopped worrying about having friends, or being fat, or following a predictable path, or trying to be a commercially sellable artist, I began to come into my own. By standing strong in my uniqueness and walking with faith in a universal, positive energy and in myself, I found my power and glory. When I was a young girl, I felt I had to push and fight for every inch. Later on, my movements as a choreographer came from a place of exploding out of confinement into freedom. What once held me back eventually propelled me forward. It took a while, but I clued in to the power of transformative magic and created a unique vocabulary to communicate it to others. Audiences understood and felt the proud, humble, unapologetic glory of my message. As I created more and took even greater risks, I came into my full power as an artist and a woman. Mia Michaels, Queen Unicorn, was unleashed.

My struggle became my friend. The abnormality turned into creativity. Creativity turned into connection. Connection gave me the life, success, and career I have now.

I didn't know it would play out this way while I was suffering through childhood, of course. Hindsight has its advantages. If I'd known at five and six that I'd learn to translate pain into power and beauty, the daily teasing and exclusion might have been easier to take. For that matter, if I'd known that career setbacks would eventually turn into cannons that propelled me forward, I wouldn't have stressed out as much between jobs. From where I sit now, I have the perspective that my uniqueness is my everything. It's where I want to live every day of my life. It's given me the friends, inspiration to make art, and the confidence to walk the streets of New York like an elegant badass banshee woman. In my profession, I defied the odds by being odd. I'm a heavyset middle-aged single straight woman at the pinnacle of success in a field that worships skinny young gay men. How did that happen? It's because I'm a loud, proud Unicorn and I wear my horn like a crown.

By accepting *your* oddness as your greatest gift:

You can take the shortcut to glory.

You can feel comfortable in your skin.

You can turn negatives into positives.

A common theme I've heard from artists and makers across every creative field—from chefs to stand-up comics, writers, and innovators—is that when you stop trying to be like someone else and doing what others expect of you, when you let go of ego and insecurity, magic finally happens.

Your life can be a magic carpet ride—you just have to make the conscious decision to live it that way. Magic is all around us if you choose to see it. Choose to be a Unicorn. Access your uniqueness and let it shine.

My father, Joe, was born a Unicorn, and he remained one until his last breath.

Like most Marlboro Men, he was struck with lung cancer and battled the disease for the better part of a year before he succumbed to it. At seventy-five, with his family around him, he spoke his final words, "Wasn't that fun? Wasn't life just so much fun? That was a great ride." I was leaning down over him when he said it, and I literally inhaled his last breath. I was in awe of the love and gratitude he expressed about his journey here and how he used his ultimate seconds on Earth to reaffirm his choice to live for fun and laughter and to the fullest in every moment. He really wrung life out to its core. It was one of the most inspiring, indelible moments of my life to date. I was crying with love and bursting with gratitude. Those three words "that was fun" were the biggest gift he gave me, other than life itself.

My mom Ruth's passing was the opposite experience for me.

After my dad died, except for going to church, she gradually isolated herself from the world. My sister and I both encouraged her to travel, to have an adventure or two. She was free to do *any-thing* or go *anywhere*. "It's time to *live*, Mom. Don't hold back in your Golden Years," I said. Instead, she stayed home alone and sank into bitterness, fear, and loneliness. She never got what she thought she deserved in her marriage, her life, and her relation-ships, she told us. Negativity seemed to accumulate inside her, and she wasn't able or willing to lift herself out of it. She was diag-nosed with pancreatic cancer a few years after Dad died.

In her final days, she was miserably unhappy, and it seemed to me she was angry with God for not healing her, despite dedicat-ing her later life to her faith as a minister. At the end, she didn't feel gratitude or joy. It was painful to witness. Mom was born a Unicorn, with her exceptional energy and outlook. She didn't get what she thought she deserved, and, I believe, negativity, fear, and unforgiveness snuffed out her spark.

From watching my parents' final moments, I saw life's choices split down the middle, between acceptance and joy *or* bitterness and resentment.

Obviously, we all want to choose acceptance and joy. But when life is hard, when you don't fit in and find yourself grasping to hang your pain on someone else's shoulders, bitterness and re-sentment look pretty tempting.

Resist, Unicorns.

When you give in to the pressure to act normal, bitterness can show up. You can fight the pressure by choosing to be as authenti-cally weird as you are, letting your horn iridescently glow. I'm not saying it's easy to stand tall in your uniqueness when your peers, teachers, and even your family tell you to suppress your true na-ture. They all agree! Are they all wrong?

Were all of my dance teachers wrong to tell me to be skinny?

You bet my big ass they were!

If doubt and insecurity dominate your thoughts, your horn could dry up and fall off. Push back against the tyranny of basic. *Love* that you have a huge, magical glowing horn sticking out of your forehead. Wear it proudly! Shine it up.

I'm grateful for every time I've been humiliated, shunned, stoned, insulted, misunderstood, and underestimated. Having survived hardships—the ones I've already told you about, and many more you'll read in upcoming chapters—is my superpower. They made my Unicorn hide bulletproof. They've reinforced my faith in myself. I've made a name for myself and love my extraordinary life. I still don't fit in, but I'm celebrated as a unique being.

All Unicorns can find happiness and success if they recognize that their differences are what make them strong and beautiful, that their uniqueness, once it is polished and defined, will attract and amaze others. Unicorns have the power to shift the universe with their passion and perspective, but only if they, like my father, choose joy over bitterness.

🦄

As you read this book, you'll explore Unicorn problems and challenges and how you can jump over each and every one of them to be the ultimate expression of yourself. My personal stories will serve as examples of what you should and shouldn't do to reach your full God-given potential in your life, loves, and passions. I'll introduce you to dozens of other Unicorns, famous and not-so-famous, who have wisdom to share about pushing yourself to new heights and consoling yourself at low points. By reading this book, your heart and mind will open up to the wonders around you and the magic and strength inside.

The truth is, none of us is "normal." We're all unique because we were made that way. "Normal" is just an illusion that Donkeys—the mainstream, the trend followers and rule enforcers—perpetuate so that they feel less afraid. Denying your individuality because you're scared, insecure, or frustrated has consequences. Fighting or hiding your true nature to fit into a standard is a recipe for depression, boredom, addiction, self-harm, and a life of extreme blandness. I've seen it happen too many times among my students. When I think of the wasted joy and creativity, because of fear, I just want to cry.

The stakes are high for Unicorns to live an authentic life. If they can do it, they have so much to offer the whole world. I can't wait to see what the future holds for people who use their gifts. With guidance and encouragement, young and young-at-heart artists can break new pavement and reimagine what's possible. Leaders can overcome social pressure to conform, turn hate into love and fear into hope. We need more Unicorns to stand up and show themselves, and we need these shining stars to take our beautiful planet into the future.

But how? How to go from Donkeyish fear and ego to the confidence and courage of a pure Unicorn?

As a teacher and choreographer, I practice tough love that yields incredible results. I can be hard on my students, but they call me Mama Mia because they know I care and that it comes from love. I want nothing but the world for them. My goal is to help them tap into their greatest potential and find their best selves. They wouldn't flock to me if I weren't validating, nurturing, and drawing out the power they already have existing inside of them.

In other words, "The Unicorn in you has got to come forward."

The first lesson I teach? On the opening day of a workshop, the students are always sizing one another up. I can see the insecurity on their faces as they compare and despair. Do they have the right clothes? The right attitude? The right look? I shut that shit down ASAP by saying, "The world worships the original. Don't look to the left or the right. Don't do what everyone else does or what you think I want to see."

When they stop comparing and are just themselves, I see a real change. It's not an easy task to guide them through it, but it's grat- ifying and miraculous to watch their discovery of self every time, as if a real Unicorn has just trotted into the room.

I hope to replicate the freedom and wonder of that transforma- tion for you as you read this book and to guide you through it.

Make no mistake: a little help is required as you begin the pro- cess of upping your essential Unicornness. Unless you've been through it already, you will have questions, such as:

What can I expect if I really go for it and just be myself?
What are the roadblocks on the Rainbow Path?
How do I mix the magical world inside my head and the nonmagical one outside it?
What if being myself makes me feel even more alone?
How do I use my uniqueness to create a joyful, unconventional life?

On these pages, I'll air out your private terrors and dreams. I know what they are, having had them myself. Often, students look at me with stunned recognition, like someone is speaking their language for the first time. It's a glorious moment of truth for them and for me, but the real magic begins when I lay out the se- crets of the Rainbow Path they're going to walk as they push their Unicorn quotient as far as it can go.

The heart of this book is the process, the journey of getting from confusion to confidence, from Donkey disguises to Unicorn pride. You have to find out and discover what *your* truth is. Your vision and instincts are what make you . . . *you.*

Along the path, you have a lot to learn and develop. I've organized the journey of empowerment into twelve steps. Each one contains all the necessary methods and strategies to make *you* even more undeniably singular and extraordinary.

Step One: Respect. You were born a Unicorn. You might not know it now, but the horn is your jackpot. Treasure and value it.

Step Two: Authenticity. To be "real," you have to stop being fake. Easier said than done in a culture that prizes #blessed and #humblebrag over genuine gratitude and humility. To polish your pure Unicorn heart, you have to banish ego and entitlement.

Step Three: Courage. Some corners of the magical forest are dark. Unicorns are often targets of bullying and they carry their hurts and scars through life. Every bad thing you face turns you into a more fascinating, evolved Unicorn if you transform negatives into positives and learn from them.

Step Four: Toughness. You will face a lot of criticism and rejection along the way, as does everyone. It's not a question of "if," but "when?" and "how bad?" You have to grow a thick hide so that insults and rejections bounce off.

Step Five: Connection. Every human being has social and emotional needs, and they can best be fulfilled by spending time with people who reinforce your best self. It's my observation that Donkeys tend to be extroverted and Unicorns are more introverted, but there are no absolutes. Even solitary Unicorns need genuine, deep, trusted friendships as well as a strong connection to the true self within.

Step Six: Fear. Use fear to your advantage. Whenever you feel your heart speed up and your palms sweat, take it as a sign you're on the right track.

Step Seven: Faith. If you don't believe, you can't jump feet first into the unknown, which is what all Unicorns must do. With faith in yourself (and God, Universal Energy, or whatever your faith is) you can make that leap. By believing in and trusting the magical/spiritual world, you can be part of it.

Step Eight: Inspiration. Unicorns are naturally curious creatures and have a bottomless thirst to listen, see, read, and travel. Learning has to be a lifelong pursuit. Seek and find inspiration to add rings to your horn every day of your life.

Step Nine: Motivation. It's not enough to appreciate art and life. Unicorns are compelled to create. Ideas come fast and furious for Unicorns, but it takes motivation to bring those ideas to life.

Step Ten: Restoration. Don't forget to stop and smell the wild-flowers every once in a while. Take an occasional mental and physical break to restore and recover, and you'll be rewarded for the rest with even more brilliant ideas.

Step Eleven: Cooperation. Although Unicorns are magical, they still have to live in the real world and deal with people. It helps to know some tricks about collaborating with Donkeys, other Unicorns, and hybrids and how to bounce back if things go to shit.

Step Twelve: Evolution. Unicorns never stop seeking, growing, and evolving, which is why your greatest years and work always lie ahead.

Unicorns, I'll teach you every single step, forward and backward, inside and out, starting with the first and most important step of all: learning to respect the gift of your uniqueness!

UNICORN: An exceptional person who revels in his or her peculiarity, despite the tremendous pressure—from parents, teachers, friends, boyfriends, girlfriends, society in general—to be just like everyone else. Unicorns shine brightest when they don't hide their inner weirdo. They don't try to look like anyone else. They don't compare themselves to other people. Their lives often start out rough. They don't fit in and that might make them ashamed at first, but they learn that being different—like, say, having a big horn sticking out of your forehead—is their greatest gift. Underneath their glitter layer is a gritty one; they are made of one part pixie dust, one part cement. No one knows what to expect from them, and that unpredictability might make people a bit nervous. Unicorns are, in fact, constantly surprising themselves and others with strange, brilliant, and risky ideas and revelations, as if they see things from a fifth dimension or through a magical lens. Their finest creative work sometimes comes from a dark place, but they trip the light fantastic in everyday existence, deriving immense joy from small things. Unicorns can't help but stand out in their originality. Unicorns can shift the planet on its axis, like Prince, Bowie, and Gaga. Being a Unicorn isn't about talent, per se. It's about having a unique, offbeat quality that they are brave enough to share with the world.

DONKEY: One who blends, a member of the crowd. Someone who goes along to get along and who feels uncomfortable veering too far from the mainstream. Donkeys believe conformity is a good thing, and they set the goal of being universally accepted and loved. Because standing out makes them jittery, Donkeys constantly judge their fashion choices, weight, and social status by comparing themselves to others. A sense of belonging is vital to their happiness, and when life circumstances drive them close to the fringe, they fight hard to get back to their safe place in the middle. They try to look like a Kardashian or a Chris (Pine, Evans, Pratt, or Hemsworth). They follow trends instead of setting them. It's not that they aspire to basicness but that the choices they make lead them to live a predictable, conventional, safe life. However, nearly all Donkeys do have a golden, magical nugget of Unicorn inside them, but it might be buried so deep in their psyche that they don't know it's there, which is a shame. If they have the bravery to fan that spark of uniqueness into a raging fire, they can overcome insecurity, fear, and ego and reach their true and highest potential.

IT'S WEIRD NOT TO BE WEIRD.

 JOHN LENNON, BEATLE

RESPECT THE HORN

ARE YOU A UNICORN OR A DONKEY?

1. Has anyone—a friend, parent, partner, or teacher—ever said to you, "Why can't you just be *normal*?" or some other variation of "Can't you be like other people?" **T or F**
2. When you tell a joke, does it make some people really uncomfortable? **T or F**
3. Have you ever dyed your hair an unnatural color or had a really strange haircut? **T or F**
4. When you speak up about something that matters to you, do others shake their heads, blink in confusion, and say, "What the hell are you talking about?" **T or F**
5. Does making small talk just to be polite about things you don't care about with people you don't really like make you want to scream? **T or F**
6. Do you believe in things you can't see, like ghosts, aliens, and pixies? **T or F**

(continued)

7. Are you a big fan of some music or art form that is on the fringe of mainstream, or do you have a very particular niche hobby? **T or F**
8. Has anyone reacted to your outfit by saying something like, "You look ridiculous," or by giving you the side eye? **T or F**
9. Has an authority figure, like a boss, coach, or teacher, described you as "a loose cannon" or "rebellious"? **T or F**
10. Are you baffled by and/or horrified by the rise of the celebrity clone culture? **T or F**

SCORING

Eight or more Ts: You are a Unicorn.
Three or fewer Ts: You are a Donkey (at the moment).
Four to seven Ts: You are a Unicorn in Donkey's clothing.

I WANT TO MAKE IT CLEAR THAT I AM NOT JUDGING anyone or saying that Donkeys aren't equally smart or good, or that they are inferior to Unicorns. Donkeys just took the message "go along to get along" too much to heart. Along with childhood conditioning and people pleasing, many apparent Donkeys are actually Unicorns in Donkey clothing. It's quite common for Unicorns to attempt to "pass" as normal—and why wouldn't they? Being different is an open invitation for mockery, bullying, jealousy, and a lot of free-floating hate aimed in their general direction. Being a Donkey seems easier, so some Unicorn-leaning people choose to obscure the horn to hide their true selves from themselves and others.

I'm not saying that Donkeys don't have problems. We all deal with human pain and snafus. We live on the same warming, warring planet. It's just that society was made for Donkeys, by Donkeys. They make the rules, and follow them, and condemn people who chafe at having to do the same. Donkeys aren't fighting an uphill battle just to be themselves. In the business world, their "groupthink" ability to conform to corporate culture and extroversion win them promotions and raises.

Unicorns, on the other hand, are born outliers. They color outside the lines. Their looks and thoughts challenge the status quo. Unicorn strangeness can be unsettling, even to family members. Unless young Unicorns are very, very lucky to be raised in an understanding, supportive family, their parents will probably do whatever they can to scrub the glitter off their hide. I don't blame parents for doing it. They just want their child to be happy, safe, and loved, and to them, that means fitting in. But teaching young Unicorns from the age of three or four that their essential nature is defective can really mess them up. They'll grow up wondering, "What's *wrong* with me?" and feel ashamed of who they are. The parents' view is reinforced in junior high, which, for the vast majority of Unicorns, is a Dark Age of teasing, bullying, and ostracism. It's amazing to me that *any* Unicorn manages to get through adolescence with her horn intact.

When you're fifteen and every force in the universe is telling you to conform or die, not doing it (by choice or because you are so odd that there is no way in hell you could pull it off) can be lonely and frightening. No one likes the idea of being an outcast. So, some Unicorns react by burying their uniqueness in Donkey covering. They aspire to be "normal," to dress like everyone else and talk like everyone else. They become followers when they were born to be leaders. Some have buried their authentic selves so deeply, they have no idea who they really are.

If this sounds like you, know these two things: (1) you are not alone, and (2) your true nature is absolutely accessible. With effort and courage, Unicorns in disguise can peel away the Donkey layers and let the horn glow. I know what you're afraid of, that when you reveal your strangeness, you'll wind up sitting alone in the cafeteria at school (actually or metaphorically). But before long, when you reach your full Unicorn strength, the glitter layer attracts people to you and makes you a standout in a *good* way. Being an original is the ultimate human freedom. A light that shines brightly illuminates the whole world. Burying it in Donkey covering keeps you alone in the dark.

IF THIS SOUNDS LIKE YOU,
KNOW THESE TWO THINGS:
(1) YOU ARE NOT ALONE, AND
(2) YOUR TRUE NATURE IS
ABSOLUTELY ACCESSIBLE.

Some Unicorns in Donkey's clothing decide on their own to ditch the disguise. Others come to a crisis point in life and have no choice but to expose their truth. Things that are supposed to go right don't. Fitting in feels more and more like a struggle that doesn't live up to its promises. The old message "believe in yourself" stops making you roll your eyes with dripping irony and starts to make sense. It'll occur to you that living a lie is choking your soul, and that maybe, if you lived honestly, it'd be a huge relief, like sucking pure oxygen after choking in a smoke-clogged room. You'll want to break out of the mold and become the person you were born to be. You don't come preloaded with peculiarities by accident. They exist so that you can use them to make your distinct contribution to the world.

Your hair isn't crazy or "bad." It's beautiful.

Your way of seeing the world isn't upside down. It's just your perspective.

Your sense of humor isn't offensive or bizarre. It's just not for everyone.

If you really think about it, why does "go along to get along" make any sense? If you want to be a positive force for change in your life or in the world, "getting along" is not going to cut it. The world cries out for leaders and creators to change things for the better, not reinforce the crappy way things are. You can be one of those people, but you have to believe in yourself first, push your own boundaries of what you think you're capable of, and then share your strength and confidence with others so they, too, can reimagine what's possible.

I'm not suggesting that we can all be geniuses like Albert Einstein or John Lennon. But we can all be the most authentic and strongest version of ourselves and bring innovation and creativity into our lives somehow in some beneficial way. Think of a viral video that is so wonderfully weird that it brightened your day, like the farmer who played the trumpet for his cows, or the mom laughing her ass off wearing a Chewbacca mask. As a society and as individuals, we crave hits of originality, creativity, and honesty. We're starving for them. A sixty-second video can alter the course of your day, or your thoughts, from negative to positive, from dim to bright. This is no small thing. In fact, it's everything.

You can choose the status quo, the same old same old, the formula, the way things have always been, the trends, the voice of controlling parents and teachers who just wanted you to fit in. If you do, you up your Donkeyness.

Or you can choose to follow your gut instincts and heart, reject the cookie-cutter version of yourself, make your own trends, and break free of routines and formulas. If you do, you will raise your Unicorn quotient.

Being an original is as simple as that: making conscious decisions minute by minute, day by day to be true to yourself. At first, it might feel uncomfortable to go the way of the Unicorn, but it'll get easier with practice. Eventually, you'll be automatically authentic and will watch in wonder as your horn grows longer, thicker, and brighter. You can actually measure it as we measure a tree's age by its rings. With each new commitment to be yourself, you gain wisdom and empowerment, and a rung on the horn.

Donkeys, Unicorns, the truth is, we were all born unique. I believe that every baby is born a Unicorn and society strips away the glitter and stunts the horn. Every single one of us is one-of-a-kind. We were all born a legend, but that doesn't mean we all die one. Ballsy Unicorns wear their horn like they won the Oscar of Life. Just by acknowledging and respecting their uniqueness, they win.

SHED ANY TRACE OF THE DONKEY LAYERS

I've helped thousands of people shed their outer Donkey. All it takes is the desire and the willingness to let it go and trust yourself.

When I teach dance, only part of that training is technical. I'm actually teaching how to shed the Donkey layer, so when students start a class with me to learn the specific steps, they are in for a big surprise. The first thing I instruct them on is self-awareness, because without that, they're just moving their bodies instead of expressing themselves with fearless, egoless, raw honesty. When your spirit dances, the body will follow. I explain the concept to a new class, and the students usually nod and say they understand.

THERE IS ONLY ONE
OF YOU IN ALL TIME,
THIS EXPRESSION
IS UNIQUE.
IF YOU BLOCK IT,
IT WILL NEVER
EXIST THROUGH ANY
OTHER MEDIUM AND
IT WILL BE LOST.

MARTHA GRAHAM, MOTHER OF MODERN MOVEMENT

They have no idea.

Next, I ask them to try a technique that strips away the accumulated layers they've piled on to protect themselves from hurt (but don't) and find the unique expression that Martha Graham was talking about.

The process is simple. I direct a dancer to stand in the center of the room, and then I ask him to "Show me who you are" and reveal his essence to me. But here's the catch: he can't *tell* me with words or a rote dance routine he knows by heart. The idea is to get a single physical snapshot, a statement without words, of who each dancer is, for them to find an image, a gesture, a posture that feels like home, that embodies their essence.

For people with a lot of doubt, pain, and insecurity, the vulnerability that the process requires can be agonizing. Their impulse is to hide in the safe place of doing what they're good at, but it won't work. Staying where you know you're fierce and celebrated is how you fail and die as an artist. I'm not asking to see their greatest hits. I push them to go deeper, to discover new insight into themselves, and then to let it out.

STAYING WHERE YOU KNOW YOU'RE FIERCE AND CELEBRATED IS HOW YOU FAIL AND DIE AS AN ARTIST.

When students find that honest position, movement, or posture, I ask them to repeat it, and repeat it, until it's locked in. It's like programming themselves to connect with their essential and honest nature. The process takes no more than ten minutes. The students start with confusion, pass through ego and fear, and, if they're brave, end with insight about who they are, which leads to a breakthrough.

Sounds great, right? Totally worthwhile!

Now it's your turn.

You don't have to be a dancer or an athletic type to do this; in fact, it's even better if you're not. If the very idea of dance feels unnatural and awkward, excellent! Because your objective is to find the uncomfortable truth, the less at ease you are, the better. You have to plow through comfortable to get to the gold of insight—and that goes for anything in life, love, business, and personal evolution—so, if you *start* in an awkward place, the experience will be that much more impactful. (For the same reason, it's a good idea for lifelong dancers to try writing their way into truth. I can tell you as a first-time author, writing is *extremely* uncomfy—and a quick route to insight for me.)

Another reason nonphysical people should try this exercise: dance connects the body, mind, and spirit and creates a flow between the breath and the heart. You can use movement as a vehicle to go deeper into yourself and into the rhythm that is bigger than you. Unicorn William Shakespeare said, "The earth has music for those who listen." Dance to Earth music, and allow something greater than yourself to literally move you. You might find that it's a welcome change to flow along rather than trying to shift the universe by sheer force of will. Freeing yourself to dance without judgement, just dance, just be who you are, is how you get out of your own way and see where your energy takes you. Remember being a child and closing the door to your bedroom, putting on your favorite song, and dancing with abandonment.

If you feel blocked by insecurity—stuck and frustrated—just start moving. Don't think, just explore. As long as you're moving in the moment, you can peel away self-consciousness and emerge

UNIQUE EXPRESSION EXERCISE: A DAILY PHYSICAL MEDITATION

1. Put on comfortable clothes and go into a private room. Shut the door.
2. Put on music that holds a special place in your heart. Close your eyes and open your ears. Just stand still, breathe, and let the music transport you.
3. Move with it. Sway, flow, and circle your shoulders. The truth comes from your guts. Start with small gestures. You will find your own movement and rhythm as you go deeper.
4. What emotions bubble up to the surface? Accept whatever ideas and thoughts rise in your mind. Don't dwell on them now. Just let the ideas flow into your head as your body flows, too.
5. Does one movement feel like home? Does it feel "right"? Flow into it, and hold it.
6. Shake out of it and move around again, until you flow back into the "home" posture or gesture. Hold it again.
7. Repeat this process of flowing in and out of a particular snapshot that feels right for you today. Repeat it. It might be a "fuck you" one-finger salute. It might be flying with raven wings. It might be looking over your shoulder at what's behind you or just hugging yourself. Own it. Know that it's where you are and what you're feeling right now, and let it inform your actions as you go through your day.
8. Do the whole process again tomorrow at the same time in the same place to explore who you are that day. If you know what's going on, and feel it in your

bones and muscles, you can prepare. If your gesture is to burst through a wall, you feel fearless, and the emotion will build. If your gesture is to rock with your head down, you are feeling isolated and protective, and know to either reach out to trusted loved ones or spend time alone, whichever is better for you. Tap in to your emotions through improvisational dance, learn from it, and then use the knowledge for strength and power.

into a position that reveals your true self. It might be like bursting out of an imaginary cocoon, or reaching for the stars, or curling into a protective ball. Whatever the struggle is, you eventually get to the point of demonstrating it in the snapshot.

Let your spirit dance and your body will follow.

THAT AWKWARD FEELING

Doing the meditation above might feel a little strange (more so than usual), which is the whole point. Discomfort is a tool for self-awareness, and fully realized Unicorns know that and welcome it. Donkeys and emerging Unicorns have to learn to embrace the unknown, to open their arms gladly to what makes them uncomfy. You will never get better at this by phoning it in. If you're just going through the motions, you learn nothing.

Unicorns welcome vulnerability. Vulnerability is the unknown place where anything is possible. In vulnerability, you lose ego and become an open vessel to receive insight, creative energy, and awareness. Your senses are alive when you're willing and unafraid to act silly and look ridiculous. Awkwardness might feel embarrassing, but inside vulnerability is freedom. One creative moment could alter the entire course of life. One bright idea, or new way of seeing things, can lead to a huge accomplishment and positive change. When playwright J. M. Barrie came up with *Peter Pan*, he faced ridicule and the judgment of Donkeys. A play about Lost Boys and fairies? A voyage to Neverland? In his imaginary world, he was beyond the reach of judgment. He just created, and his dream became the blueprint of imagination for generations. To allow that spark to ignite you, you have to maintain a state of welcomed vulnerability—open, alive, and ridiculous. Just like the creativity of a child's mind.

UNICORNS WELCOME VULNERABILITY. VULNERABILITY IS THE UNKNOWN PLACE WHERE ANYTHING IS POSSIBLE.

Donkeys, on the other hand, are controlled by insecurity. Insecurity is the known place where nothing is possible. Insecurity is living inside your bad history of judging yourself and shutting yourself down. All the things from childhood that pushed your buttons—feeling unloved, ugly, fat, stupid, powerless, foolish— can take over your mind and block creativity and empowerment. If you are so insecure that you're unable or unwilling to open your heart and look like a fool, you won't break through to the extraordinary. The fear of being judged slams the door on magic.

DONKEYS, ON THE OTHER HAND, ARE CONTROLLED BY INSECURITY. INSECURITY IS THE KNOWN PLACE WHERE NOTHING IS POSSIBLE.

DON'T BE A HALF-ASSED UNICORN

Not to imply that Donkeys are full asses! Although, ass *is* another word for Donkey. . . .

Half-assed people say things like, "I don't care. Whatever you want is fine." They start projects and don't finish them. They can't decide what to wear. They say things like, "I'm not sure how I feel."

What is behind being half-assed? Do people genuinely have no opinion about what they eat, wear, see, do, and feel?

My belief is that indecision is a way to hide your true feelings from others so that they won't judge you if they disagree. A deep Donkey is determined to be just like everyone else, and having a strong divergent opinion just won't do. To play it safe, Donkeys say, "Whatever you want," or they just nod in agreement.

Every deferred or self-censored idea and opinion piles another layer of Donkey clothing on a Unicorn's back. Being half-assed and indecisive is not the way to become a legend.

BEING HALF-ASSED AND INDECISIVE IS NOT THE WAY TO BECOME A LEGEND.

Now, a person who *always* loudly expresses how he feels is what's known as an ass*hole*. An asshole tries to cram his or her opinions and ideas down other people's throats. Assholes make demands instead of offering suggestions. They are hiding, too, by using aggression and intractability to cut off any ideas or opinions that don't mesh with theirs. They're afraid of anything that challenges the status quo. Assholes might think of themselves as

original. But they're really extreme Donkeys who follow by leading other followers.

Unicorns are not half-assed *or* assholes! You can up your Unicornness by speaking up if you have something to say, laughing
because you think something is funny, saying, "I'm not fine, and
it's not perfect" because you are upset and trust that a loving person won't reject you for having a negative opinion and strong feelings, even if that has happened to you in the past. The Unicorn
ideal is to revel in being yourself and when appropriate to express
your distinct opinions with as much respect for others as you have
for yourself. Sure, ten people might sneer at you. Two or three will
applaud you. Even if no one does, applaud yourself.

Set a daily intention of clueing in to your genuine feelings.
Start small. Are you hungry? Are you tired? Do you have something to say? Is there power in silence? If you can train yourself
to know how you feel about little things, you'll gain clarity about
bigger, harder things, too. You don't have to be the center of attention of others if you give plenty of it to yourself. When I'm in
a room, I don't waste the oxygen of speaking if I have nothing to
say, but I'm always listening and considering.

PRINCE AND ME

Several years ago, I collaborated with the Purple One on a tour to
be performed by him and one other dancer. He invited me to Paisley Park, his Chanhassen, Minnesota, compound to work there.
One Friday night, the female dancer and I were rehearsing in the
studio. It was late, around two in the morning, and I thought everyone else was gone. All of a sudden, we heard a ruckus of crash-
ing and banging. The dancer and I looked at each other and
decided to investigate. We followed the noise by creeping through

WE DANCE FOR LAUGHTER,

WE DANCE FOR TEARS,

WE DANCE FOR MADNESS,

WE DANCE FOR FEARS,

WE DANCE FOR HOPES,

WE DANCE FOR SCREAMS,

WE ARE THE DANCERS,

WE CREATE THE DREAMS.

 ALBERT EINSTEIN, POET

hallways until we came to the indoor theater where Prince and his band performed. (Paisley Park also had an indoor basketball court, two recording studios, a sound stage, a sewing room for his custom costumes, and a vault for his master recordings and memorabilia.)

The dancer and I snuck into the theater and hid behind the door. Except for one single spotlight, the space was dark. The legend himself was in a circle of light, on the stage, shirtless, in his usual high-heeled boots and tight, stretchy jazz pants. He was playing a guitar, incredible riffs on another level. Then he put down the guitar, ran over to the drums, and whaled on them, the ultimate solo. Then he put down the sticks and rushed over to the piano, going off on that for a while. The entire time, his eyes were closed tight. He was in a creative, artistic frenzy. His energy and passion seemed inhuman, like he was being controlled by a force greater than himself.

It was the most incredible artistic expression I've ever had the good fortune to witness. He looked like the God of Music, or as if divine energy was coursing through him. Remember, it was the middle of the night. Prince's creative time was in the dark hours, another unusual characteristic, and he was known for that quirk. If you collaborated with him, he would call at two or three in the morning and say, "Let's go!"

He was one of the great King Unicorns of my life, a man who had no choice but to be himself and to let his purple light shine. Forget his legacy in the music industry; just his existence gave baby Unicorns permission to explore their uniqueness and sexuality, to say, "Prince wears eyeliner, heels, blouses, and jazz pants and doesn't care what anyone thinks. Maybe I can dress or act however I want, too."

Everything about that man was special, from his talent, to

his looks, his work ethic, and his genius. Our collaboration took place over a short period of time, but it made a huge impact on my life that I take with me forever. If I ever need a reminder of what it means to be myself, respect my uniqueness, and never take my gifts for granted, I think of him. Thank God for Unicorns like Prince who have the courage to share their genius with the world and make us see things in a different way. Life would be so boring without them.

As a Unicorn, go ahead and be grateful for *your* uniqueness. Thank your parents, your mentors, your pillow. Thank God every day that you're not basic, even if you have to put up with a lot of crap because of it. The Unicorn life is not always rainbows and butterflies. The enchanted forest can have cloudy skies and falling meteors. You can weather any personal storm by holding tight to your golden center, your authentic self.

Your horn is your life preserver.

It's the greatest gift you have ever been blessed to receive.

It's your strength. With it, you can push through walls that keep pushing back.

It's a compass, showing you how to navigate through life.

The horn is a constant reminder to move forward. Once you hurdle rocks on the Rainbow Path, they are behind you forever.

The horn never lets you forget how awesome you are.

YOUR HORN IS YOUR LIFE PRESERVER.

No matter what your life is like *right now*, be glad you were born you. Be thankful for the horn of plenty, the gift that never stops giving. If you're lonely, be grateful. If you're confused, be grateful. If you're fucking pissed off, be grateful. No matter the challenges, you are ten steps ahead because you are smart enough and brave enough to be grateful for your greatness. Say "thank you" through the pain and "thank you" through the joy. You'll have plenty of both, so you might as well revel in every experience, learn from it, and use it as fuel for creativity.

THE UNICORN CONTINUUM

By now, you understand the difference between Unicorns and Donkeys.

Unicorns stand out by being unusual and are not afraid to let their weirdness shine, like Freddie Mercury of Queen, a man who, like Prince, was extraordinary in every way, from his looks (his mustache, overbite, bottomless brown eyes, and tall, lanky body) to his flamboyant taste in fashion (lots of white studded jumpsuits that showed off plenty of chest hair), his distinctive voice (instantly recognizable in a couple of notes), and his mind–boggling originality as a songwriter. "Bohemian Rhapsody"? Has anyone before or since put together a rock song that is so jam–packed with surprises? If he'd written just that one song, he'd have been a King Unicorn for all time. But he wrote dozens of unforgettable tunes, including "We Are the Champions," a raw, proud celebration of the triumph of tenacity and owning your victories, mistakes, your whole wonderfully weird self.

Or consider the exalted Unicorn genius Albert Einstein, a man whose brilliance was so far above the realm of mere mortals that he was able to come up with the theory of relativity and prove how time bends in space. Do you have any idea what that actually means? Join the club! Quantum mechanics. $E = mc^2$. Atomic theory. There was so much energy and electricity in his brain, it made his hair turn white and stand up! His very name has become a synonym for genius.

Unicorn Meryl Streep is a fucking brilliant actress who can make you laugh, cry, or sit on the edge of your seat. Talk about someone who never copies herself! I think the reason she takes so many roles with foreign accents in so many genres is just to see if she can pull it off. Streep's characters are so varied, she's running out of acting risks to take, but I'm sure she'll find more and conquer them because, as an Extreme Unicorn, she simply can't stop testing herself with new challenges.

We can't all be as beautifully strange as Prince and Mercury, as brilliant as Einstein, and as versatile as Streep. They are diamond-studded Unicorns, the stellar examples of human creativity and brilliance who could never have lived ordinary lives (and why on Earth would they have wanted to?). They can be found on the far, far left end of the Unicorn-Donkey Continuum.

On the far right end, you'll find the most extreme cardboard-cutout generic Donkeys, who wouldn't know an original thought if it bit them on the ass. I'm sure you can come up with examples of cardboard-cutout Donkeys. I think of them as basic bitches and bullies from junior high, all grown up, mediocre, uninspired, and boring as hell. Extreme Donkeys, people who have no spark, no ambition, no curiosity or creativity, are just as rare as diamond-studded Unicorns.

Picture the continuum like this:

Most of us fall somewhere in the middle. Where would you put yourself? Smack dab at the midpoint? Closer to the Unicorn side? Closer to the Donkey side? Granted, very few of us are pure diamond-studded Unicorns. It's common for people to veer Donkey in some areas, and veer Unicorn in others.

For example, say, you're a typical working mom in the suburbs, carpooling your kids to school, paying the bills, living a so-called normal life. But in your spare time, on a whim, you start writing a novel about a college student who meets a mysterious, wealthy, sexy man and has an intensely erotic affair with him in his leather bondage dungeon. You take a chance and post some chapters on a fan fiction website, and before you know it, you are the author of a global phenomenon that has been credited with bringing BDSM erotica into the mainstream.

E. L. James, author of the Fifty Shades of Grey trilogy, is still in shock about the success of her little hobby. Before she started writing, she might've stayed farther toward the Donkey side of the continuum in her suburban mom existence, baking cookies and driving carpools, but when she let her freaky, black-leather dark side out for a trot, her Unicornness shifted to the far left side of the continuum.

Or, say, you're a young woman who suffers from depression. You decide to create an alter ego as a kind of therapy to deal with your feelings. You give that alter ego the name Superwoman because when you were a shy little girl, you pretended that you had an invisible S on your chest when you felt scared. Superwoman becomes the star of a YouTube series. The stories evolve to include other characters—parents, teachers, friends, all played by you in wigs and costumes—and are so funny, people start watching them. Before you know it, they've been viewed 1.5 *billion* times, you've written a book, made a feature film, done a comedy tour, and won awards from MTV and Nickelodeon.

Superwoman, aka Lilly Singh, started out as a depressed shy girl looking for some relief, and now she's the most popular female YouTube celebrity *of all time*, galloping from the middle of the continuum all the way to Extreme Unicorn.

Where do you put yourself on the continuum right now?

Do you stand in your uniqueness, or do you hide what makes you wonderfully weird?

Do you take risks creatively and personally, or do you play it safe?

Are you striving to be authentic, or do you make decisions based on how you've done things in the past or by what other people think you should do?

WHERE DO YOU PUT YOURSELF ON THE CONTINUUM RIGHT NOW?

DO YOU STAND IN YOUR UNIQUENESS, OR DO YOU HIDE WHAT MAKES YOU WONDERFULLY WEIRD?

If you place yourself closer to the Unicorn side, *great*. You are confident in your originality and can use this book to get even more *un*comfortable and grow your horn to obscene lengths.

If you place yourself closer to the Donkey side, also *great*. You have learned something powerful already: that you have a lot of room to grow and evolve into your true self.

It doesn't matter if someone looks at you and sees a cardboard-cutout Donkey. You might not look like a true original. So what? You can be a true Unicorn on the inside even if you're conventional on the outside. In some ways, being consciously conventional in the looks department has its own authenticity and is therefore Unicorny. A few years ago in a fashion movement called Normcore, people dressed so "normal" it was weird. It so was! You'd see people with polyester pants and button-down short-sleeve shirts, and think, "Wow! That's so bizarre!" (Eventually, it became a trend, and therefore Donkeyish, but I applaud whoever started it.)

It only matters what you think of yourself.

The continuum is a scale. You can move around on it depending on the choices you make. Ask yourself, "How can I be more Me today? How can I push the Unicorn *Meter* closer to Extreme Unicorn in this conversation, in this class, in this task, in this hour of free time?" What options do you have to take yourself further into who you really are, down deep, underneath those Donkey layers, to the core of your one-of-a-kind soul?

You have the chance in nearly every decision you make—during a typical day, you will make thousands of them—to be more honest, creative, driven, more essentially *you*. All it takes to slide the scale is a little push. You don't have to know how you'll realize your Unicorn potential yet. All you need to do at this point is *want* to move your life, thoughts, and behavior in a more truthful and original direction.

Inching closer to the Unicorn side might happen just by saying, "I want to be more ME, even if I don't know exactly what that means."

INCHING CLOSER TO THE UNICORN SIDE MIGHT HAPPEN JUST BY SAYING, "I WANT TO BE MORE ME, EVEN IF I DON'T KNOW EXACTLY WHAT THAT MEANS."

The thing about learning who you really are and what you're capable of is that you always start in confusion. How can you know who you are unless you've taken steps to find out?

Elevate your Unicorn quotient this very second by saying, "I have no freaking idea what is going to happen next." Saying "I'm lost" is how you'll eventually find yourself.

THE KEY

Use the key to respect the horn and unlock your inner Unicorn:

You have to believe it before you can be it. Do you believe you were born a legend? Are you aware of what makes you unique? Do you believe that there is some part of you that is unlike anyone else? The point is to be mindful about your choices and to always ask yourself, "Is this *really* who I am?" Don't hold back in whatever areas and ways you are different. Freeing your originality in one aspect of life likely unlocks other areas.

ALWAYS BE YOURSELF,
EXPRESS YOURSELF,
HAVE FAITH
IN YOURSELF,
DO NOT GO OUT
AND LOOK FOR
A SUCCESSFUL
PERSONALITY AND
DUPLICATE IT.

BRUCE LEE, MARTIAL ARTIST

STEP TWO

PURE OF HEART

IF THIS BOOK HAS ONE GRAND, EPIC GOAL, IT'S to help you become the most distilled, pure, true version of *you* possible. Or, in other words, the Unicorn's prime objective is authenticity.

Authenticity is a word that gets thrown around a lot, but that doesn't necessarily cheapen it. To me, it means, simply, being yourself. As a Unicorn, you must always be asking, "How can I be more my honest-to-God self today?" The answer is always: listen to your heart, guts, and instinct.

The trouble is, authenticity is a bit of a jellyfish—transparent yet slippery. It's hard to get a firm hold of the very concept. If you *are* yourself, then why do you have to remember to *be* yourself? I've found that it's easier to grasp authenticity from an inside-out perspective: How are you *not* yourself? Are you wearing a mask to appear to be someone other than who you really are? Does anything you do contradict your essential nature?

An inauthentic Unicorn doesn't exist. Donkeys with strap-on horns *do* exist, however, and are the people who think they're "truth tellers" and "keeping it real" when they couldn't be more fake and unsure of themselves. You see a lot of this breed on reality TV (trust me, I've been there).

People often sample false personas from a young age and, to some extent, trying on different "hats" (or horns) is a natural part of figuring out who you really are. I tried out a few personas along the way and made authenticity progress by realizing those experiences were definitely not me!

Figuring out who you are (and who you aren't) is a process. A shortcut is to start with labels and "types" that you're familiar with. For example, I always seem to get hung with the "artsy" label. Ask yourself:

How did I get my label?

Did someone label me and I decided to keep it?

Do I think being that type is cool and I made myself into it?

Is my label by default because jock or brain or nerd doesn't fit?

A lot of the labels and types we grow up with turn into habits and default assumptions we make about ourselves. They might be accurate, but then again they might be 100 percent Donkey shit. Contemplate how comfortable you are with yours. If they feel like a good, safe fit, then immediately THROW THEM OUT. *Comfort* and *safe* are Donkey words. If you're snug and cozy in your labels, you are not exploring the depths of your soul. As a Unicorn, you have to scratch away the surface personas to get to the glitter of truth underneath.

Who are you?

What lies do you tell yourself about yourself?

How is your head buried in the sand?

Do you make assumptions about what you can and can't do on the basis of what other people have told you is possible?

Just some good questions to ask yourself. Put them in your pipe and smoke it.

ENEMIES OF AUTHENTICITY

Two factors make it nearly impossible to live an authentic life: ego and entitlement.

Ego is thinking you're "special" and having a worldview that is centered around yourself only. Egomaniacs are smug and self-satisfied and believe they are more important and better than everyone else and that they have arrived.

Entitlement is feeling like you deserve everything in life, even if you haven't worked for it. If you don't get what you want, you feel deprived or like you've been cheated.

Of course, Unicorns *are* special, and they do deserve all the joy and wonderment of the world. You have to walk a tricky tightrope between overconfidence and awareness that the world doesn't owe you a damn thing. In this age of instant gratification, no one wants to work or wait for the gold. They think it should be handed to them just because they showed up. Unicorns know (or learn) that they are responsible for making their lives and painting their masterpieces.

QUIZ: HOW LOUD IS YOUR EGO?

Answer the following questions as honestly as you can:

1. If you work hard and play by the rules, you deserve comfort and success. **T or F**
2. If you treat others fairly, you can expect them to treat you the same way. **T or F**
3. You know that you are smarter and more talented than you get credit for. **T or F**

(continued)

4. If things go wrong for you, it's probably someone else's fault. **T or F**

5. If you don't get what you want, you have every right to sulk about it. **T or F**

SCORING

If you answered any of these questions with a T, you have some work to do to quiet your ego, the voice that says the world owes you everything. There are no sure things in life, including love, success, wealth, or joy—even for the so-called deserving. You can work hard and do your best to tip the scales in your favor, but even then, there are no guarantees.

Understanding this basic truth makes dealing with setbacks and disappointments a lot easier. You won't waste as much time and energy on being upset, resentful, and feeling cheated and can zoom right back into Unicorn mode, doing your best, having honest, from-the-heart intentions, and cultivating an attitude of gratitude about whatever good fortune you experience.

CHECK YOUR EGO

Some people stumble on the Rainbow Path because of overconfidence. It is possible to have too much of a good thing. The downside of excessive ego is that: (1) people will hate you, (2) you'll promise more than you can deliver, (3) you won't push yourself to take risks and grow because you think you're so fantastic already. Deflate a ballooned ego by repeating these truths:

1. **"I am replaceable."** Presidents are replaced every four or eight years. Julius Caesar, the emperor of Rome, was so expendable his senators stabbed him to death. If you think no one can take your place, remember that someone else was there before you. Someone else will be there after you.

2. **"I don't know."** Even if you are an expert with five advanced degrees, you do not know everything about your subject and a million others. It's simply not possible to know everything. Thinking you have learned all you need to learn is like building up a brick wall in your mind. A Unicorn isn't embarrassed by not knowing. In fact, not knowing and being excited by curiosity to learn are pure Unicorn.

3. **"I don't deserve it unless I work for it."** You have to work hard and strive to get what you want. In the real world, there are no medals for showing up. Free lunches are a Donkeyish delusion, so learn to expect nothing, and you'll be thrilled with what you earn.

IN MY HUMBLE OPINION

Being pure of heart starts with **humility**. What does humility mean? It's knowing that you are no better than anyone else; no one else is any better than you. You are not "above" anything or anyone. Unicorns need to be willing to humble themselves and do whatever it takes to gain experience that will bring them into their own. To soar to new heights, you have to be low to the ground. In U2's "She Moves in Mysterious Ways," Bono sings, "If you want to kiss the sky, you better learn how to kneel." Seal sings, "In a sky full of people only some want to fly. Isn't that crazy."

Be honest about the work you do and how you undertake it. I tell dancers to move with a pure heart, and the body will follow.

The same is true for living a happy life. Do things for the right reasons—and be honest about what those reasons are.

Don't take shortcuts, or you'll miss out on the wisdom of going the long way. Don't do anything for praise or applause, or you'll never create something truly wonderful, which would be humbling indeed. And don't "fake it till you make it" even though the entertainment industry would say otherwise. Any fakeness slides your Unicorn Meter toward the Donkey side. If you don't know what you're doing, research it, learn by doing, have the courage to ask for advice and guidance, and shift into Unicorn mode with passion, energy, and curiosity.

HUMILITY CLASS

When I arrived in New York in my early twenties to make a name for myself as a choreographer, I went straight to the biggest commercial studio, the Broadway Dance Center on West 45th Street, and tried to get a job there. I was qualified, having been a teacher for some time already, but the director said there weren't any positions available. I wasn't going to give up that easily. If I couldn't work inside the studio, I'd get as close to it as I could, so I took a job in the dance supply store right next door. I sold leotards and slippers to prima donna bunheads who gave me attitude and treated me like the rosin on the bottom of their toe shoes. I watched with envy as the dancers went into the studio for the classes I couldn't afford. I could only swallow so much pride, though. After a few months, my job ended in a fury when a ballerina yelled at me for getting her the wrong shoes and called me (surprise!) fat. My inner banshee warrior reared up, and I threw a pair of toe shoes in her face.

I didn't like that job anyway. After I got fired, I walked immediately back into BDC and pleaded with the director for any job at

BE YOURSELF. EVERYONE ELSE IS ALREADY TAKEN.

 OSCAR WILDE, WIT

all. She took pity on me and let me join the scholarship program so that I could take classes in exchange for cleaning the studio at night. So began my illustrious career in scrubbing toilets. I would have done anything to be there and was devastated when the program ended and my money ran out. I had to go back to Florida to regroup and got right back into teaching kids at my family's studio, the very job that I'd tried to run away from to pursue my dream.

Not long later, I found my way back to BDC, thanks to Frank Hatchett, a legendary master jazz teacher who'd seen my choreography through the years at competitions. I trained my students there like little ninjas of movement, superheroes in training, and deep artists, with one clear goal: put something new out there and have your own voice. We were disqualified from a lot of competitions by breaking the time rules and presenting unconventional and controversial content, but we didn't really care. Trophies would have been nice, but making an impact, changing lives, and getting standing ovations were better, and I loved that everyone left frazzled by our performances. Frank Hatchett liked what he saw of my work and asked me to come back to New York to substitute-teach his class at BDC while he was away. I appreciated this opportunity all the more for having been humbled by New York before, and I worked that much harder to prove I belonged. My real career started during this time.

During that second stint at BDC, I realized that after so much rejection as a dancer, I would create my own world as a choreographer. If I was going to shift the universe of dance and have a place in it, I'd have to start my own company, so I did. RAW (Reality at Work) was my baby. With no financial backing, we were given free studio space at BDC between two and six a.m., and we danced our hearts out in the wee hours every single night (morning). When you force yourself to create when you'd rather do anything else, you wind up breaking new ground. I look back at that time as an explosion of discovery as a young choreographer, like the universe was opening up to me in every way—except financially. Every cent I made teaching went into RAW. We stayed together for four years, a roller-coaster ride of successes and disappointments, until we finally called it quits and went our separate ways. No regrets, though, for all the blood, sweat, and tears—and money—I poured into my company, which was, for me, a master class in humility.

From age nineteen to thirty, I paid my dues and then some. I was chronically broke and exhausted, but every time I pushed past my preconceived limits, I upped my Unicorn quotient and my dreams became clearer. My horn grew rapidly and was the beacon that lit the way through those uncertain years. I never lost focus, vision, or hope.

THE HUMILITY PARADOX

You know when performers win a big award, and then they go up on stage and say how "humbling" it is?

I don't get that.

Are they humbled to be standing up there in front of their talented peers with a golden statue in their hands because they think they suck? Because they are no better than anyone else at that moment? Or is it just a "humble brag," something to say because they think celebrating without reservation would seem like sore winning?

To get to that level of success, you have to work your ass off and devote yourself to the job 1,000 percent. Some people get lucky breaks. Some are born with an abundance of undeniable talent. But most people get the award (or the raise or the promotion) because of dedication and determination. Instead of feeling humbled by kudos, celebrate them! Life doesn't hand you glory too often, so when it does, don't minimize it by downplaying it. Go ahead and toot your Unicorn horn, loud and proud. Celebrate!

I've won three Emmys for Outstanding Choreography on *So You Think You Can Dance* and many other awards and honors over the years. Hearing my name called, walking to the front of the room, and accepting a shiny hunk of metal put wings on my feet. I was thrilled, excited, and grateful—and, yes, humble. The other nominees were equally deserving, but I won, and such an experience does make you stop and think, *Do I really deserve this honor?* During the five minutes between hearing your name, doing your speech, and walking off stage, you run through a dizzying gamut of emotions, but then you wake up the next morning and you're still the same person you were before the win. You go back to doing what you do every single day of your life: counting your blessings, earning your oxygen, and being grateful for every moment of your beautiful and crazy life.

Of course, on the big night when I'm acknowledged for hard work I've done previously, I celebrate the moment of glory while remaining my usual grounded-yet-ethereal self, ever striving to take the work I'm currently doing to the next level.

I'm proud of my Emmys, but I don't sit in my office and gaze lovingly at them lined up on the shelf. Just like my bank account, my apartment, my weight, or my friends, my awards are not a measure of my worth. My most valuable possession is my Unicornness. I'm privileged with self-awareness, self-love, and self-acceptance. Awards are nice, but receiving one is not the end of the story. I look at the evidence of past successes and say, "Today, I haven't even started yet." I won't settle for Emmys. I think, *Got that, now on to the Tonys and the Oscars.*

My dreams keep me hoping and working. As soon as you rest on your laurels, you're not in the thick of creativity. I've never fully loved anything that I've created so much that I was truly humbled by my own brilliance. I liked moments of my work, but I've loved more that my work has helped and inspired people. That's what brings me joy. Next time, maybe the true brilliance is going to come out. That kind of thinking is a blessing and a curse. It's what keeps me going back to the studio for another try.

LISTEN TO YOUR GUTS

I don't mean stomach rumbles or gas.

Back in Step One, I asked you to scrub off your Donkey layer by dancing into a unique expression that felt like home.

It's time to try a new experience to learn to stop listening to your ego and to tune in to your true instinct instead. When you listen to your ego, you rely on your brain, what you "think" is right. Personally, I believe that thinking is overrated. If I think things through every time I have to make a risky decision, I wouldn't take a chance on the new and exciting. Rationality is inherently a cock blocker sometimes.

Instead, I listen to my heart and my gut and let my instincts lead the way. Unicorns are intuitive creatures, and if you're able to put ego aside and stop overthinking, you can actually hear the inner voice that tells you straight up what you *really* feel and what course to take. At first, it's hard to trust what your instincts tell you—we all get stuck in our habits and learned behaviors—but you will get better at it and will come to see that your gut is a better life guide than your brain.

Here's another meditation to try whenever you aren't sure what you should do about any kind of quandary, minor or major.

THE GUT LISTENER: A DECISION-MAKING MEDITATION

1. Sit on a chair or on the floor of a quiet room, close your eyes, and ask yourself the big question of the moment, like, "Should I take this job or start this new project?" or "Should I break up with him?"
2. Listen to your brain. What is it telling you? If you're deciding whether to take a new job, for example, make a list of logical pros and cons in your mind. What are the reasons for taking it? Are they superficial factors like money, fame, or ego fulfillment? What are the cons? That the job might be too hard or not exactly what you imagined?
3. Now *trash that list*. Imagine yourself ripping it up and flushing it down the figurative toilet.
4. Picture yourself taking ten giant steps away from logic.
5. Listen to your gut. Aim your thoughts into your belly. Do you register a churning anxiety? Are your guts quiet and calm?
6. Listen to your heart. When you visualize yourself in the new job, does your pulse quicken, or do you get a bad feeling?
7. Open your eyes and write down on a real piece of paper whichever course of action made you feel intimidated and frightened.
8. Accept it is the one your gut and heart want you to take.

When I sit down to have a talk with my instincts, I interpret an anxious stomach and a racing pulse as signs that point to yes. Doing things that scare you means excitement, a challenge, a new adventure. If your guts are calm and your heart rate is steady, that means the job is a safe, uninspiring choice. It might be a good choice—for a Donkey. But Unicorns have to push themselves away from safe and into the frightful place where true creativity and learning happen.

Seek the place of being nervous, *but not reckless and dangerous*. For instance, I'm speaking at Harvard University as the keynote speaker at an arts conference. I'm terrified, but I have to do it to see what I'm made of and to push the boundaries. There's a difference between public speaking to educate and to take yourself to the next level and setting your car on fire to see what will happen.

THE KEY

To unlock authenticity:

Live for the butterflies. When those wings start flapping in your stomach, it's your gut sending you the message, "This idea scares the living crap out of me! I better look into it." Your guts and your heart are the voices that guide you toward excitement and risk, what Unicorns eat for breakfast. It's all about authenticity: if you aren't a little bit terrified, you're not figuring out who you really are and what you're capable of.

SOMETIMES
PAINFUL THINGS
CAN TEACH US
LESSONS THAT
WE DIDN'T THINK
WE NEEDED
TO KNOW.

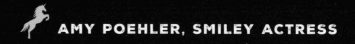 AMY POEHLER, SMILEY ACTRESS

STEP THREE

SOME CORNERS OF THE FOREST ARE DARK

LIFE CAN BE ROUGH ON UNICORNS. I'M NOT GOING to sugarcoat it. You'll have to pass through lots of heartache and doubt on your way to radiance and happiness.

As I mentioned, when I was in Catholic grade school, I was teased and bullied constantly. The other kids hurled a steady bombardment of insults at me, calling me "retard" and imitating my gait. I was taller and stronger than the other kids, including the boys. To kids that age, different is frightening. They think odd is contagious. Fittingly, my classmates avoided me like the plague.

I said to myself, "Okay, they don't want me in their world, so I'll make my own over here." (A common sentiment of mine.) During recess, I sat under a tree, strumming a guitar and singing to myself, or I danced while the other kids either ignored me or gawked in disbelief—at first. But then, curiosity got the better of some of them. One or two would tentatively wander over to me, sit down, and ask if they could try the guitar. More of them came to see what was going on, and before long, a couple of the kids showed up at school with their own guitars or other instruments, and we'd all play together under the tree.

Don't get me wrong, it wasn't all sunshine and love from then on. They still didn't seem to like me; no one was inviting me over after school for playdates and milk and cookies. But in the universe I created under the tree, I was their fearless leader and they looked to me to choose the songs and to conduct the makeshift orchestra. We were eventually the group that sang at all the church services in my Catholic school.

My dad used to say, "You *are* a leader, Mia, not a follower. Accept that leading is what you were born to do, even if that means you don't have a lot of friends. The captain of the ship is always the loneliest."

But it got harder to do that. This was around the time when I started taking flak from dance instructors about my size; they told me repeatedly that I shouldn't bother pursuing my dream to be a ballerina because I was just too fat, and I listened.

"You could be a great artist if you were thinner."

"People don't want to look at fat dancers."

"The rule is, you have to be thin. You aren't following the rules."

Apparently, there was a Bunhead Code of Conduct, and its first tenet was "All ballerinas must be fragile, swanlike, and delicate."

Even Dad used to say, "You would be so beautiful if you would just lose some weight." He told Dana and me, many times, "It's not about how you feel. It's all about how you look." How messed up is that? Dad, the ex-model, had his own issues, clearly. It just goes to show you that even a deep Unicorn like my father can get stuck in some Donkeyish sensibilities out of his own insecurities.

I was always trying to lose weight. Like an obedient little windup doll, I made a serious stab at anorexia and ate only one bowl of oatmeal per day for an entire week. That was the worst week of my life! I thought about food and eating constantly, and when I started eating again, I inhaled big bowls of pasta and gained all the weight back and then some, and was promptly accused of self-sabotage.

I was born to be a powerhouse, able to move heavy furniture as a toddler. I wasn't born to be a waif, but I was blamed and shamed anyway for not being one. I mean, how dare I *eat?* Did I want to destroy my future with *food?*

The weight issue was, and still is, a real problem in the dance world, with so many girls developing eating disorders and so many more wishing they did! Whenever I see dancers with a raw, hungry, and desperate look, I just want to give them a hug and a burger. I know what they're going through, the internal and external pressure they're under. My heart really breaks for the chubby dancers, too, who always stay in the back row and gaze enviously at the sickly, skinny girls around them. They are so smothered by the insecurity of being overweight that they can't let the artist free. Sometimes, it seems like everyone is at war with him or herself.

I get it. I've been there; I've suffered. And I want you to know that whatever form your pain takes, you can take it into your body and, with a little bit of effort, transform it into rocket fuel to launch yourself a million miles away from heartache. I pushed past the weight, and when I danced, I felt stronger, more free, and at my most powerful.

HOW TO SHUT DOWN BULLIES

As bad as bullying was during my school years, it's much worse today because of social media. Laws and regulations have been put in place to stop taunting in schools, but there's only so much that can be done online. Twitter is a haven for anonymous haters and a war zone for everyone else. This is the reality of our world. There are strategies to cope with it, in real life and online.

1. **Get some perspective**. Bullies loom large in your mind because of the intensity of pain they cause, but actually they represent just a tiny fraction of *all* the people in your life. If you have three hundred Twitter followers, and thirty post anonymous insults, that means only 10 percent of them are knuckle-dragging Neanderthals. If you go to a school with a thousand kids, the two jerks who give you a hard time represent 0.2 percent of your classmates. They are loud, yet tiny. Don't narrow your big, beautiful world by letting a few bullies loom larger than they really are. Focus on the positive people and connections in your life, the goals you want to accomplish, the things that give you joy.

2. **Bullying is so *their* problem**. What motivates bullies? Why are they such assholes? Most likely, it's one or a combination of these three things: (a) they're insecure and trash you to feel better about themselves, (b) they're attention hogs, and (c) they're trying to transfer their pain onto someone else. I'm not saying you should feel sorry for your nemeses, just don't take their harassment personally. Yes, they're attacking you, but it's not about you. You didn't put the hate inside them. It sucks a lot that you have to bear the brunt of it, but you are not respon-

sible for it. Although having insight into bullies won't make them stop being horrible, it might give you some satisfaction to know that they're probably even more fucked up and sad than you could ever be.

3. **Give them blue balls.** Deny them the satisfaction of getting under your skin. If they bully you for attention, ghost them. They don't exist. You don't see them, you don't hear them. Ignoring bullies is like cutting off their oxygen. Bullies expect you to crumble, cry, feel like shit about yourself, or fight back. If you feed trolls red meat, you only make them stronger. Starve them.

4. **Agree with them.** Maybe you *are* fat. Maybe you are a nerd, or a slut, or a freak. So what? You have every right to be yourself, to love yourself for who you are, for all of your quirks, desires, interests, and appetites. If bullies try to insult you by calling you what you already know you are, it's just an observation. It's your choice to feel shamed or insulted by it. Whatever the taunt is, tell yourself, "Well, duh, I am fat. I'm also kind, smart, funny, creative." Don't let bullies define you. Define yourself!

5. **Always respect the horn.** If you are the target of bullies, it's because you stand out. Something about your looks, attitude, style, or vibe is different from the mainstream. Being different strikes fear in lesser minds, and they will lash out at someone whose unusual style, looks, and attitude disturb them. At the heart of all bullying is the Donkeyish insecurity that results from confrontation with Unicornish uniqueness. In a way, bullying is confirmation that you are doing something so strange and so awesome that Donkeys can't handle it. Don't give in to their insecurity and narrow-mindedness by shutting down. Keep on pushing boundaries and expressing yourself.

PAIN IS A GIFT

Lady Gaga was tormented as a kid. "[I was] teased for being ugly, having a big nose, being annoying. [People said] your laugh is funny, you're weird, why do you always sing, why are you so into theater, why do you do your make-up like that? . . . I used to be called 'a shit,' be called this, be called that, I didn't even want to go to school sometimes," she told *Rolling Stone* in 2011.

"Some of the girls in my class were hanging out with some boys I knew also," she described in a video interview. "I went to meet some friend [there], and the boys picked me up and threw me into a trash can, on the street, on the corner of my block where all the girls could see me in the trash. Everyone was laughing. I was even laughing. I had that nervous giggle and I just remember holding back the tears and the lip quivering, [thinking] *don't let them see you.* One of the girls looked at me and said, 'Are you about to cry? You're pathetic.' That's what I felt. I remember not telling my parents because it was too embarrassing. It didn't sink in with me how much bullying affected me until later in my life, and how much it was still very present. It took see[ing my fans'] struggles to unlock that in myself. The fans were the key to unlock what I did want to address that made me a greater songwriter."

Lady Gaga eventually used her uniqueness to become a superstar and an outspoken advocate for underdogs and misfits via her Born This Way Foundation. Her dark history shaped her creativity, and eventually she turned it into a benefit for other Unicorns, too.

OWN YOUR WHOLE LIFE,
EVEN THE UGLY PARTS

A strange or rough childhood is not a requirement for creativity, but, let's face it, hurt helps a person peel away the bullshit and experience raw, honest emotion. Being bullied is practically a rite of passage for young Unicorns. It's the awful gauntlet you have to run to get to self-love and empowerment on the other side.

I urge my students to explore their darker and edgy personal histories, the parts of life that they'd probably like to forget. The nooks and crannies inside dark, awkward places are where genius lives. Get uncomfortable with those emotions and their residue, and then pour it all into creativity. Link the past to the present. See who you are, who you were, and who you might become. The good times and bad times are mixed together to create your masterpiece: your life. Tell your story fearlessly and unapologetically. The world needs to hear it in whatever vehicle you choose to use.

THE NOOKS AND CRANNIES INSIDE DARK, AWKWARD PLACES ARE WHERE GENIUS LIVES.

The patron saint of "going there," celebrating and examining your dark past, is the poet Maya Angelou. If you don't know much about her life, here's a quick snapshot:

She was born poor in St. Louis to parents who were so dysfunctional and unfit, they shipped her off to her grandparents in Arkansas when she was only three. After four years as a displaced kid, Angelou's father appeared suddenly and took her and her brother back to St. Louis, where she was sexually assaulted by her mother's boyfriend a year later. Her rapist was basically set free despite being found guilty, and four days after his release from jail, he was killed, presumably by Angelou's uncles. After the killing, she was shocked mute and didn't speak for five years. Her parents once again sent their daughter to live with her grandparents, where, in her silent world, she developed an excellent memory, observational skills, and a love of books. She made another move, this time to Oakland, California, with her mother, where she had a son at seventeen and supported him by becoming a table dancer, prostitute, and madam.

The incredible woman who wrote all those amazing poems and books, who was a US *poet laureate*, a civil rights leader, best buds with Oprah Winfrey (another vocal victim of child abuse), once was a hooker. Angelou never kept her dark past a secret. In fact, she wrote the memoir *Gather Together in My Name* about her history as a sex worker to find meaning in her ordeals and to share them so that young, troubled readers wouldn't feel ashamed or guilt-ridden about their desperate acts, whatever they might be. She used her *whole* life in her art and mined each trauma for insight into her experience and the larger human condition. Her hardships solidified into strength, and she went on to become one of the most respected and revered women in the world. No matter how you start in life or what happens to you along the way, if you use every morsel of emotion and experience for good—and really own and explore all of it—there is no limit to what you can become and how you can change and affect the world by being simply you. Wear all your scars as artwork.

ALAN AND ME

One of my favorite people is Alan Cumming, a talented actor in *The Good Wife*, *X-Men*, *Spy Kids*, and *Cabaret* on Broadway, to mention a few of his credits. Our agents put us together to collaborate on a project, and we clicked at first sight. It was an instant Unicorn Connection. We wound up spending the whole day together, hand in hand, just two Unicorns escapading all over New York City. I loved Alan's spirit, his little secretive laugh, his mischievous eyebrows, and the way he looked at the universe. He saw worlds of colors and details that he pointed out to me all day as we walked the streets; then we went to a photo shoot for a magazine, a movie premier, and finally a glitzy party—it was a fantastic, glittered-and-laugh-packed day. I met Alan's husband at the party that night. He walked in to find us sitting on a couch together, thick as thieves, as if Alan and I had known each other our whole lives, not just ten hours. Alan's husband asked, "Who is *she?*" and we just started laughing.

Growing up in Scotland, Alan was beaten, humiliated, and demoralized daily by his father until he left home at eighteen to go to college. Through his art, he figured out how to turn his childhood pain into a positive. He wrote in his book *Not My Father's Son* that he wouldn't know joy if he hadn't lived with anguish for so long. As an actor, he uses his wide range of emotions to play offbeat roles and transforms his misery into a stellar career just being Alan.

DOMINOS

I'm giving you all these examples of people, myself included, who embraced their pain to show you how life is one big domino effect. Today is not what you think it is. It's a piece of the larger puzzle of your life. One day, you'll look back and be glad for what you've endured because it made you who you are (or who you will be one day). On some level, you're not surprised by your struggles because you were not meant to have an uneventful life. You are being tested to prepare you for what you will become. When I look back, it is all so clear that I was a banshee wild Unicorn, born to walk a different walk, to live outside the mainstream—and I always knew it.

I bet you know it, too.

I've made peace with my demons—every kid who excluded me, every teacher who called me fat, every director or producer who tried to tame me—because I know they added rungs to my horn. It was confirmation that I must stand in my truth and never compromise.

You are majestic, whether you realize it yet or not. When you tap into the majesty, you can take out the garbage, aka all the negative emotions and hurtful memories that rot inside you. By saying "I was meant to have those experiences in order to become myself," you can turn junk into gold.

Not getting what you want, not being perfect, not having it easy is the story of every Unicorn I know. Life isn't easy for anyone, but only a Unicorn can say, "Perfection as a goal is pointless." Pretending everything is perfect is boring, fake, and a lie. When you allow yourself to be imperfect—and honest—you are living your truth. You are beautiful for what you've been through, perfectly imperfect.

WHEN I WAS LITTLE, I WAS
TOLD THAT I WAS DIFFERENT
AND I FELT OUT OF PLACE,
TOO LOUD, TOO FULL OF FIRE,
NEVER GOOD AT FITTING IN.
AND THEN ONE DAY, I REALIZED
SOMETHING: DIFFERENT IS GOOD.
WHEN SOMEONE TELLS YOU
THAT YOU ARE DIFFERENT,
SMILE AND HOLD YOUR
HEAD UP AND BE PROUD.

ANGELINA JOLIE, BUTTON PUSHER

TURNING A NEGATIVE INTO A POSITIVE

When I was fifteen, I was one of thirty kids chosen to perform throughout Miami as part of an elite arts program. I'd given up ballet by then. I was twice the size of those girls and had accepted the reality that tutus and toe shoes weren't a good fit for me. But I could do modern/jazz dance, a style that suited my physicality more than ballet anyway. During our training, the teacher sized up her team. When she got to me, she gave me the once-over and said, "Mia. You'll never really make it in the dance world. You're just too big."

This *again?* I was humiliated and hurt—and furious at this teacher. Why did she choose me if she had a problem with my size?

Our first performance was at an inner-city elementary school in front of a crowd of around a thousand kids. The skinny ballerina group performed their routine first. They were graceful, predict-able, traditional, and well tolerated by the restless audience. Then, the powerhouse, muscular jazz/modern girls in our blue unitards came on stage . . . and the entire audience laughed at us. I was so confused by their reaction. Was it our costumes? Our nonballe-rina bodies? Our dance moves? Clearly, we didn't fit their con-cept of "dancer," despite being strong and well-rehearsed. They responded by laughing at us. It was mortifying for all of us, but I was the only one who was so embarrassed that I ran off the stage, headed straight for the bathroom, and hid in a stall, even jumping up on the toilet so no one could find me.

The humiliation of that day knocked me off my game for a while. I was young, and all the criticism about my body and the audience's reaction were too much for me. So I stopped dancing altogether. Eventually, though, I gained insight into the experience and recognized it as a nudge from the cosmos to explore all the ways I could be involved in dance, and that led me to choreography. I went back into the studio and started creating routines from my point of view for other people to perform. My goal had been to be a dancer first, but because of all the rejection, I turned to choreography, which was a more natural fit for me.

Looking back, I see that one of the reasons I've been successful as a choreographer is *because* of my unconventional dance body. My style of movement is inspired by physical power, gravity, and my rebel warrior athleticism that conceals a huge, mushy heart inside.

When I get the occasional flashback "I wish I were lighter" pang, I remind myself that God gave me a big ass for a reason. I take pride in what once caused me so much doubt. If I'd stuck it out as a dancer, and starved myself successfully, my career wouldn't be where it is now and I wouldn't have inspired the world by telling my story as a choreographer. My career has no built-in time limit. I'm still evolving and growing every day.

That was a dark, insecure time for me, and back then, the darkness served me creatively. But as I get older, it doesn't serve me, nor do I want it in my life. My goal is to constantly move toward the light.

Though not every problem can be turned into a positive with a change of perspective, many can. What you think of as an obstacle might wind up being what propels you to where you want and need to go. Respect every aspect of your uniqueness, even the parts you hate. Don't ask, "How can I change myself to look like everyone else?" Ask, "How can this so-called problem work to my advantage? How can I be inspired by it?"

Turning a negative into a positive is a puzzle—one of many on the Rainbow Path—that only you can solve for yourself. Here are the stories of how my student and my friend did it:

CASE STUDY 1: **Maggie**, an artist and musician, told me, "I'm a very sensitive person. I cry easily and take things to heart. I've been self-conscious about it because I was raised by tough parents who hated it when I cried or 'overreacted' or acted 'irrational.' They would say, 'What's wrong with you?' I thought that my sensitivity was a flaw that would always come between me and happiness. But then I realized that I could use that emotional intensity and channel it into my art to make it more meaningful and impactful. So whenever the feelings well up inside me, I don't try to stop them or hate myself for having them. Instead, I grab my guitar to write a song or pick up a sketchpad and draw it out. I made the connection between sensitivity and productivity, and it's been working for me ever since. Turns out, there's nothing 'wrong' with me. My sensitivity is something right."

Negative: Extreme emotional sensitivity.
Positive: Channeling intense emotions into artistry.

CASE STUDY 2: **Alice** is a mezzo in a New York opera company. As a girl, she dreamed of singing the soprano parts, playing the frail ingénue in her favorite operas. But, like me, Alice was born to be a powerful warrior woman, a real Valkyrie. She sized up the situation very early and realized she'd never get to play the soprano parts even if her voice was brighter and more colorful than those of the other women auditioning. So she decided to train her voice to sing a little lower and auditioned for the meatier mezzo parts— there's one in every opera. She wouldn't get to fall in love on stage, but so what? Her goal was to have a career as a singer, and her size and powerful voice won her roles she can age into. At forty-five, she's an in-demand mezzo, whereas a lot of the sopranos she came up with have been replaced with younger, prettier versions.

Negative: Being the wrong "type."
Positive: Working with her type instead of against it.

UNCONVENTIONAL = BEAUTIFUL

The world has enough gloss and fakeness and so-called perfection. Trying to look like the "Hollywood standard" is striving for generic, interchangeable, boring cookie-cutter basicness.

Imperfections, on the other hand, are the most beautiful, memorable aspects of people. I see loveliness in what's real: a funny nose, a chipped tooth, a broken heart. People who celebrate their unconventional looks, and who actually become icons of beauty and style because of their so-called flaws, elevate their Unicornness. Anyone can do it. Apply the same principle of turning a negative into a positive. What's your most distinct feature? Make it your trademark.

Khoudia Diop, twenty-one, comes from Senegal. When her family moved to New York, she was called names like "darky" and "daughter of night" because of her ebony skin. She fought back by confronting the bullies for their racism and by loving her looks. Her Twitter handle is @MelaninGoddess (melanin is the pigment that makes skin dark), and her following is more than 350K strong. She's become a role model for self-love—and a fashion model, too. She recently told *People*, "Self-love is an ongoing process and practice. I've had to sit with myself, learn myself, find the things I like about myself, and celebrate them. This is how I've recovered from the aggressive negativity sent my way." She summed it all up by saying, "We are all Goddesses."

Shaun Ross, twenty-six, an albino black man with a misshapen nose, was a complete freak growing up in his Bronx neighborhood. He was called "Powder" and "Casper" for his pale skin and light-orange hair. "I've always felt like an extraterrestrial lifeform trying to find its way back home," he once said. His unusual looks caught the attention of admiring Unicorns, and as a teenager, he danced for Alvin Alley and modeled, appearing in British *GQ*, Italian *Vogue*, and *Paper* magazine, and walked the runways for Alexander McQueen and Givenchy. He has also performed in music videos for Katy Perry, Beyoncé, and Lana Del Rey, among others. His one-in-a-billion face is featured in Ford's "Be Unique" campaign. Again, what caused his pain in childhood is now his career and calling card.

An unconventional beauty I just love is Sarah Jessica Parker. People seem to pick apart her features, but all I see when I look at her is a striking beauty and the elegant way she presents herself to the world. She celebrates what she's been given and enhances it with confidence and innate style. I respect her for being a creative, a wife, a mother, and a woman over forty in Hollywood who produces and stars in her own shows and for her self-love that comes from within and makes her majestically beautiful.

UNICORNS AND ADDICTION

Some Unicorns rise above the bullying, demons, insecurity, and challenges. And some succumb to them, and numb or escape their pain with drugs and alcohol. Addiction has taken so many of us: Amy Winehouse, Kurt Cobain, Elvis Presley, Janis Joplin, to mention a small fraction of the tragic club.

When I was in high school, I hung out with the druggies, Goths, and tattoo freaks—the outsiders, like me—in the parking lot of the local skating rink. Quaaludes were the drug of choice among my crew. A few nights I came dangerously close to being arrested or dying because of stupid choices I made. After one close call, with the wrong people, taking the wrong substances, I sobered up and returned to the dance studio for the first time in a year or so.

The temptation of oblivion is always going to be there, but instead of being addicted to a substance, get addicted to substance. What is the gold of life for you? What fills you up and sustains you? For me, it's creativity. I get higher by challenging myself at work than I do by taking any drug. The only way to push your Unicorn Meter is to be more yourself, but when you're high all the time, you have turned yourself over to the drug. I'm not going to judge you or preach to you, but if you want to be the best person you can be, it's simply not going to happen if you're addicted.

But you already knew that, too.

THE KEY

To put rough times into perspective and use them to your advantage:

Pick up your invisible shield. For every negative, there's a positive. For every down, there's an up. For every problem, there's a solution. Unicorns who embrace and stand in their uniqueness, see their differences as gifts, and veer toward the light of positive thinking, self-love, and compassion will find the protection and comfort they need to go forward in life and amaze the world.

I USED TO THINK I WAS THE
STRANGEST PERSON IN THE WORLD.
THERE MUST BE SOMEONE JUST
LIKE ME WHO FEELS BIZARRE AND
FLAWED IN THE SAME WAYS I DO.
I WOULD IMAGINE HER, AND
IMAGINE THAT SHE MUST BE OUT
THERE THINKING OF ME, TOO.
WELL, I HOPE THAT IF YOU ARE OUT
THERE AND READ THIS AND KNOW
THAT, YES, IT'S TRUE I'M HERE, AND
I'M JUST AS STRANGE AS YOU.

FRIDA KAHLO, ARTIST, ICON

STEP FOUR

HIDE OF STEEL

AS YOU ALREADY KNOW ONLY TOO WELL, UNI-
corns are sensitive creatures. We take things to heart and feel
criticism deeply. If only we could brush off criticism as just one
person's opinion, not to be taken too seriously. But, instead of
flicking it off our shoulders like lint, Unicorns sink into criticism—
even constructive criticism that's supposed to help.

Earlier, I encouraged Unicorns to trust their instinct and not
use logic to make important decisions. When you judge feedback,
however, logic is a better guide than emotions. To add rungs to
your horn and grow a thick hide of steel, consider your sensitivity
quotient first.

QUIZ: HOW SENSITIVE ARE YOU?

1. An art teacher gives your painting an A but makes
   one niggling technical suggestion about brushstrokes.
   Instead of feeling great about the grade, you obsess
   about the side comment. **T or F**

(continued)

2. If a partner makes an off-hand remark about your jeans making your ass look beefy, you consider burning the jeans and breaking up with your partner. **T or F**

3. You go to a movie with a friend and absolutely hate the film. Your friend, who considers himself a film buff, loved it. If he says, "You don't know what you're talking about," you feel ashamed to have shared your opinion. **T or F**

4. Your boss calls you into her office to criticize the quality of your work. You are so freaked out by the meeting that you can't concentrate on what she's saying. When it's over, you run to the bathroom to cry. **T or F**

SCORING

If you circled *any* Ts, your skin is too thin right now. But that's okay! You're here to change and, for you, that means growing a bulletproof hide so that slings and arrows literally bounce off of you. This chapter will help you put criticism into perspective and teach you strategies to feel stronger about how to criticize yourself productively so that you can continue to learn and evolve and add rungs to your horn.

WHAT DO *THEY* KNOW?

I once saw a movie that was a huge hit, which the Hollywood hype machine called the Greatest Film of All Time.

I should have known it would suck.

Hated it! HATE. It was painful to behold. Okay, the cinematography was pretty. But the plot and the acting came off, to me, like a disposable, bland, trifling "entertainment product" from start to finish. There was nothing original, authentic, meaningful, axis shifting, or pavement breaking about it. The plot didn't stay with me longer than the taxi ride home. Not that every movie has to be deep and dig down to the marrow of your bones—we all need mindless diversion on occasion—but to compare this trifle with movies that aim much higher and resonate in our minds and hearts for years is a crying shame and an insult to quality filmmaking.

But that's just my (always humble) opinion. You are free to agree or disagree with me about this, and anything in my book. Why? Because my judgment is no more or less valid than anyone else's. If you told me that this movie filled *your* heart with pure joy, good for you. You had fun at the movies. I won't judge you for liking it, we will respectfully disagree, but I'm not going to change my mind because you or the Oscars say otherwise. My taste hardly ever matches up with the mainstream anyway. #Unicornproblems.

When someone insults you, criticizes you, or tells you that your opinion is "wrong," don't react defensively or shrink away from your feelings. If you give what I think of as a crappy movie two thumbs up, then own it! A Unicorn has a visceral reaction to art, and all judgment comes from that deep place. The Donkey move would be to disavow your true feelings just because someone tells you to. It's also Donkeyish to stubbornly stick to your guns, no matter what, even after you've been enlightened by someone else's valid criticism. As always, it's all about learning: learning to have faith in yourself, and learning from wise and worthy others.

As a Unicorn, you have another tightrope to walk between being sure of your feelings and allowing your opinions to evolve as you gather more information. Join the conversation by speaking your mind *and* listening with both ears open. Sharing your thoughts is a gift. If you give yours, graciously accept it when others reciprocate. If the person you're talking to has nothing to offer, then you can politely end the conversation or change the subject. You don't have any time to waste "hearing out" idiots. Time is the greatest gift of life. Use it wisely. You can't get it back.

AS A UNICORN, YOU HAVE ANOTHER TIGHTROPE TO WALK BETWEEN BEING SURE OF YOUR FEELINGS AND ALLOWING YOUR OPINIONS TO EVOLVE AS YOU GATHER MORE INFORMATION.

REJECTED!

Rejection, like most things that won't kill you, builds character and thickens your hide. Every time you move forward after a "We regret to inform you . . ." letter or an "I'm just not that into you" text message, you'll be stronger for it. I won't sugarcoat the fact that rejection feels like a punch in the gut, but when you recover from the blow, you stand a little taller and a little stronger (after the "fuck you!" goes away).

In 2015, Meryl Streep told the following story on the *Graham Norton Show* about auditioning for an Italian movie producer to play the object of King Kong's lust in the 1976 Jeff Bridges's remake of the classic monster movie:

[The audition] was [with] Dino De Laurentiis senior. His son had seen me in a play and so I went up to the top of the Gulf + Western Building, the 33rd floor. . . . He had an amazing office that looked all over Manhattan. I walked in and his son was sitting there, very excited that he'd brought in this new actress. [The father] said to his son in Italian, *"Che brutta,"* [which translates as] "Why do you bring me this ugly thing?" It was very sobering as a young girl. I said to him in Italian, "I understand what you said. I'm sorry I'm not beautiful enough to be in *King Kong.*"

This story resonates with me for so many reasons. First of all, I know only too well how it feels not to get the part or the job because of one person's subjective assessment of your looks. She must have shocked and embarrassed the hell out of the producer by answering him in his own language. As a struggling young actress trying to break into film, she had the gumption to put an older male movie producer in his place with just one sentence. Priceless. No wonder she's still telling this story forty years later.

Meryl didn't let that dismal audition stop her, of course. A couple of years later, she landed a supporting role in *The Deer Hunter* opposite Robert De Niro that paid $35,000, which must have seemed like a huge amount. The movie was a hit, she became an overnight sensation (although she might object to the "overnight" part)—and she got her first Oscar nomination. Since *The Deer Hunter*, she's been nominated for an additional seventeen Oscars and has won three times. Her fee has gone up a bit since 1978, too, and is usually in the $5,000,000 range.

No one needs a reminder that Meryl Streep has had a long, wildly successful career. So has Jessica Lange, then a model with no acting credits, who got the *King Kong* part. If Meryl had given up after being called "ugly," the whole world would have been deprived of her talent. If Jessica Lange quit acting because *King Kong* was, reportedly, a nightmare to shoot, we would have been deprived of her talents as well, seen most recently in her fantastic portrayal as Joan Crawford in the TV series *Feud* and the beloved *American Horror Story* series.

The point is that judgment and criticism, whether fair and accurate or biased and bullshit, are out of your hands. You can't control what other people—peers, friends, bosses, admissions staff, book publishers—think of you. You can only control how you react to their judgment. Remember, it's not about them or what they think. It's about how you handle rejection.

Meryl chose to speak up for herself and walk out of there with dignity.

Dr. Seuss, J. K. Rowling, and other famous authors reacted to rejection with persistence. Hard as it is to believe, *Harry Potter and the Philosopher's Stone* was turned down by twelve publishers. Jack Canfield's *Chicken Soup for the Soul* was rejected by 140. Beatrix Potter couldn't find a publisher for *The Tale of Peter Rabbit*, so she self-published what is now a timeless classic. Stephen King's *Carrie*, John Grisham's *A Time to Kill*, Frank Herbert's *Dune*, Nicholas Sparks's *The Notebook*, Alex Haley's *Roots* were all stamped "REJECT!" by dozens of publishers. And yet, the authors persisted, and they got their work out to readers, who have been gobbling up their stories ever since.

It doesn't matter if you get a hundred no's. It only matters if you get one enthusiastic yes. I think rejection can be even more powerful than acceptance because it spurs you to realize your dreams. Each no pushes you one step closer to yes. I think this is why so many successful people save and even frame their rejection

LISTENING IS EVERYTHING.
LISTENING IS THE WHOLE DEAL.
AND I MEAN THAT IN TERMS
OF BEFORE YOU WORK, AFTER
YOU WORK, IN BETWEEN WORK,
WITH YOUR CHILDREN, WITH
YOUR HUSBAND, WITH YOUR
FRIENDS, WITH YOUR MOTHER,
WITH YOUR FATHER.
AND IT'S WHERE YOU
LEARN EVERYTHING.

MERYL STREEP, CHAMELEON

letters, a combination "Fuck you" to the rejecter and "Look at me now, bitches!" last laugh.

HOW TO TAKE A PUNCH

To push your Unicorn Meter, always think about how an experience can work to your advantage. To turn rejection into a gold mine:

- **Savor it!** Unlike most people, you had the balls to put yourself out there, and a rejection is proof of your courage.
- **Consider the source.** Who is making the negative comments? If it's a blowhard know-it-all, disregard. If it's a rival, the judgment might be meant to make you look bad and make them look good in comparison. The insulter might be someone close—a parent, a partner, or a colleague—with an emotional agenda. Just be aware of the why of the remarks before you take on the what.
- **Weigh it.** When I ran off the stage at that Miami event after the audience laughed, I was being controlled by my emotions. Unicorns are emotional creatures, and that's a net positive, but those powerful feelings can make you blind and deaf to forces that are trying to nudge you toward radiance. Not *all* critics— from "truth-teller" friends to demanding teachers, critical parents, bosses, and partners—are doing it to be mean or because they're jealous. Some are genuinely trying to help by giving you a new perspective or their honest opinion about what is and isn't working. Of course, you could be way ahead of your time, and their opinions might be 1,000 percent wrong. But always weigh the possibility that you could learn something

valuable from people you respect. A Unicorn strives to put hurt feelings aside, just for a few minutes, and to ask, "Is this criticism valid? Can I use it to improve? Can I make a solid case against it?" Weighing criticism objectively (meaning, without emotion and defensiveness) is its own kind of genius.

- **Trust.** Too many times in my life to count, a rejection closed the door on one project, freeing my time to take another job that, in the end, was a better fit and took me to new creative horizons. If you don't get the job or the date, it's because you're meant to be available for something or someone else. If the parking space is occupied by a Kia, how can a Benz park there?

JUDGED FOR JUDGING

I was a choreographer on *So You Think You Can Dance* for eight seasons, but during tryouts and for my final season on the show, I became a resident judge. As you know, my job was to sit on the judge's panel and critique the dancers and their performances. The dancers always worked so hard, and I usually praised their artistry and effort. But there were a few times when my honest opinions were taken as unfair or mean-spirited by the dancers, the other judges, the fans, and the media. I learned a new lesson: *You can be harshly judged for judging.* Unfortunately, complete honesty is not always appreciated.

In one season, I was a bit rough on a dancer I'll call EyeRoll. Because he came from the Miami dance world, I had very high expectations of his abilities and professionalism.

His potential? Good, not great as far as I could see yet. He had skills, but when he performed, I found his style to be powerful and masculine, yet lacking in maturity and fluidity. In my opinion, he didn't seem to connect with the movement on an emotional level, and that didn't resonate me.

What really pissed me off was his attitude. I'm very old school about respecting the art, craft, your peers, and your choreographer, and I saw his "I'm special" ego and "I deserve this" entitlement. As a judge, I wanted to be honest, so I told him how I felt about the attitude he was bringing. As you probably guessed, it didn't go over well.

My objective was to be honest and scare him a little so he could check his ego and entitlement, but my tough love tactics weren't appreciated by him or the other panel members. One of the other judges was so upset on the dancer's behalf by what I said, she nearly cried! Eventually, I explained my frustration with him, and he respectfully set out to correct his attitude.

In another season, I took a harder hit for speaking my truth. My critique of one dancer set off an Internet firestorm. I called his Bollywood routine unfocused and flailing and said that I didn't particularly enjoy watching it. It seemed like a fair judgment of his effort and his level of expertise. He was talented, but he had a ways to go in terms of his artistry. The next day, I faced a savage rebuke of my criticism on fan blogs and Twitter.

An avalanche of negativity came at me online, seemingly out of nowhere. From my perspective, I'd done the unfortunate, difficult job of telling a dancer what he didn't want to hear, that he could be better. The other judges agreed with me, but I guess my way of expressing disappointment was harsher than theirs. If I believed someone was phoning it in, I reacted by questioning his or her commitment and integrity. On that day, he wasn't very impressive, and I said so. That was my job.

Part of my shock at the reaction was that, so far on the show, the fans seemed to appreciate my honesty. Not this time. I felt like something had turned, and I was suddenly being punished for what had earned me praise before. People were digging to find a reason for my criticism other than the one I'd plainly and clearly expressed. Complete strangers were trying to turn me into someone I'm not.

What I learned from this whole experience is the importance of words and how you have to choose them wisely and deliver them with care. As a choreographer, on and off the show, I have always called it like I see it in real time. I express my opinions, suggestions, and frustrations honestly. My goal is to improve a dancer's performance, and make him or her a great artist. The only way to do that is to praise what's going right and correct what is problematic. I could have been more diplomatic about how I delivered my thoughts on a performance and could have taken more care not to hurt someone's feelings. Lesson learned. I'm working on my mouth and my delivery. Still not perfected yet.

My feelings have been trampled a thousand times in this business—and I've got a hide of steel to prove it. I've learned plenty about how to savor and weigh harsh judgments of my work. But during my time as a judge, I realized I could learn a few things about dishing it out. After that rough week, I took a step back and thought about the impact of my words. I apologized to the dancer on the next show and said that it hadn't been my intention to hurt or offend him, and that I was sorry if I had. He accepted my apology, and the show went on. If I could go back in time and judge him for that dance all over again, I would have taken him to task, but with slightly softer words that would help and not hurt. Lesson learned.

THE HARSH TRUTH ABOUT CRITICISM

No matter how much the truth hurts, it's always less painful than a lie. This applies to whether you are getting it or giving it. The most important criticism you will ever give or receive is from yourself about your own work. Look at it objectively by keeping your emotions out of it, a discipline with a high degree of difficulty for Unicorns. The way I do it is to create from the heart with pure emotion, and then edit as if the work were made by someone else. As weird as it might sound, an objectivity trick is to put yourself in the third person, so instead of using "I," use your own name while tinkering, as in, "Mia Michaels really screwed up there. Not good enough. I better fix it." Actively search for weak spots and react by strengthening them. The best way to hunt for flaws is to use your instincts. If you get a sinking feeling in your gut about an aspect of your work, or a moment of cringe, it's a message from your subconscious to change, edit, improve, or just cut it.

THE MOST IMPORTANT CRITICISM YOU WILL EVER GIVE OR RECEIVE IS FROM YOURSELF ABOUT YOUR OWN WORK.

Telling yourself that your work is perfect only perpetuates the lie that you can't aim higher. Everyone can work harder. Every project can be improved. If you know you've done all you can, ask yourself ad nauseam, "How can this be *even better?*" Take steps to fix it to your liking, make it the best you can, and then you are above judgment. The harsh words of others can't hurt you. If it's the best you can be and do, you should be happy and proud of yourself.

THE KEY

To grow a hide of steel:

Be tough on yourself. Be your own worst critic and demand excellence in everything you do. But also know when to pat yourself on the back and give yourself a break.

WE ARE ALL A LITTLE
WEIRD, AND LIFE'S A
LITTLE WEIRD, AND
WHEN WE FIND SOMEONE
WHOSE WEIRDNESS IS
COMPATIBLE WITH OURS,
WE JOIN UP WITH THEM
AND FALL IN MUTUAL
WEIRDNESS AND
CALL IT LOVE.

 DR. SEUSS, POET

STEP FIVE

FIND
YOUR BLAZE

JUST AS WE CALL A GROUP OF LIONS A PRIDE and a family of whales a pod, I call a gathering of Unicorns "a blaze," because hanging with like-minded, positive friends can start a raging fire of creativity. You don't need many friends, and you might have trouble making and sustaining friendships. I, for one, have been more of a loner my whole life; however, I have found pockets of people who have become lifelong comrades. I've had many temporary, intense, short-term friendships and relationships that served a purpose.

Some Unicorns don't feel comfortable in large groups, and our social needs are small—much smaller than party animal Donkeys—but we are human and do need comfort and support. It's essential for Unicorns to find their small tribe, their blaze, the few friends they can count on, while also appreciating that the most important comfort of a Unicorn's life is the fire within, the inner voice and self-love that sustains.

HOW TO FIND FRIENDS

Some Unicorns may never be popular, but popularity is mean-ingless, so don't bother worrying about it. The process of finding your blaze is instinctual, but that doesn't make it easy, especially when you're young and lonely.

Because Unicorns are often misunderstood, they're not going to attract a multitude of fans at school, but they also have a way of locating their kind. It's almost magnetic. You are literally pulled toward someone who will "get you." As you inch closer, your horn will glow brighter and brighter.

A writer friend of mine said, "You'll find coal and charcoal in the same place. But only some of the chunks can turn into dia-monds. In any group, I look around for the one person who sets off my radar, and zero in on them." It might turn into an instant Unicorn Connection from day one (like the moment Alan Cum-ming and I met for the first time), or it might turn into a Unicorn Conflict, which happens on occasion, too. (Later, I'll tell you an epic "Clash of the Unicorns" story.) Know that just because some-one is a Unicorn doesn't mean he or she is friendly or trustworthy. Proceed with caution.

You can hedge your bets about finding your blaze by living in or near cities with a dense Unicorn population. Do you have to move? Maybe. One day. If you live in a place where Unicorns thrive and are appreciated, you up your chances of making great friendships.

QUALITY OVER QUANTITY

Your blaze might be three people, or it might be just one—a Uni-corn can be her own best friend. You don't need a hundred BFFs or even a dozen to be happy. If a Unicorn can count her true, trusted friends on one hand, she's got all she needs.

During most of my childhood, I had a couple of friends. The one time I was part of a larger friend group was during my partying days when my loneliness delivered me into the wrong crowd. As an adult, I have my very few lifelong friends who are in it with me in such a profound way. I've always prized quality over quantity, knowing instinctively that having those one or two people who understand and encourage me is enough outside support for me to have the confidence to be my optimal self.

Rare true friendships are easy and organic. When you're together doing something exciting like traveling or banal like making pasta, your soul is nourished with laughter, a feeling of being "seen," mutual appreciation, and encouragement. You feel more alive and healthy with this person for as long as he or she is in your life—which might not be forever, so treasure every moment.

Some soul matches last your whole life, and some continue for only a few intense months. As meaningful as they are, Unicorn friendships can be temporary. I've noticed that people come in and flow out of my life. Sometimes the leaving results from a conflict or because we just don't operate on the same vibration. I used to feel sad when I grew apart from someone I once loved, but now I appreciate the connection for what it was. We learned what we needed to learn from each other and then went on our merry, separate ways. Every person comes into your life for a purpose, although it might not be apparent what that reason is until years later. If the friendship is intense, then the influence will be significant somehow. I wouldn't be who I am if I hadn't been close with the diverse array of people, the cast of characters that has changed and shifted, as I do, over the years.

A Unicorn's grace is being grateful for new influences and connections.

A Unicorn's wisdom is learning what you can from each other to evolve and grow.

A Unicorn's power is letting go of relationships that have run their course.

UNICORN CONNECTION

Is there such a thing as Unicorn Link at First Sight? I believe there is, and it happened to me with none other than Tony Bennett.

I have to start my Tony story by going back in time, to when I was around ten.

My mom and I were in Orlando for a dance competition. At the convention hotel, we rode the elevator. It took us up to the penthouse to pick someone up. Two men walked on, a big one and a little guy. The smaller man said to me, "Hi, what's your name?"

"Mia," I said.

"Are you a dancer?" he asked.

"You bet your sweet ass I am!" Well, I didn't use those exact words, but I was enthusiastic.

He put his right hand on my left cheek and said, "You are adorable. What a face!"

The elevator dinged, the doors opened, and the two men left.

My mother, meanwhile, was totally freaking out. "That was Frank Sinatra!" she raved. "Frank Sinatra touched my daughter!"

I had no idea who he was, but apparently he was in town for a concert and was staying at the same hotel.

Flash forward to 2016. I was having dinner with a friend at Rosa Mexicana by Lincoln Center when suddenly a man walked in to the restaurant and people started applauding. We turned to see who it was, but everyone had stood up and was blocking the view. All I could see was a full head of gray hair and tan skin.

The man and his entourage moved deeper into the restaurant and closer to our table, and I saw that it was Tony Bennett. He was smiling illuminatingly, and he was so charismatic. You couldn't help but leap to your feet and clap just being near him. He looked over in my direction, and our eyes linked. I felt an instant Unicorn Connection with him, and sure enough, he made a beeline for our table. He introduced himself to me, and then put his right hand on my left cheek—just like his crooner contemporary had done forty years earlier—and said, "What a beauty! God bless you."

Same hand, same cheek, same message.

Then he walked away, and I couldn't speak for the next five minutes, thinking about the touch of Frank and Tony on the same cheek. What did it mean? Why was I touched by these men? I don't have an answer; perhaps it's just an acknowledgment of Unicorn by Unicorn.

Frank was famous for his blue eyes. But, having looked into the eyes of both men, I think Tony's eyes (also blue) are even more remarkable. His shine with kindness; his spirit is bursting with life, energy, light, and joy. There's such a sense of fulfillment in them.

Keep your eyes peeled for an instant Unicorn Connection, and you will probably find one. I'm not saying it'll turn into an epic friendship or romance, but merely tapping into that vibration is an amazing experience worth searching for.

SHOULD UNICORNS HANG OUT
WITH OTHER UNICORNS ONLY?

Any of my close friendships with Donkeys have always felt like work. They were more soul sucking than nurturing, and I eventually realized that I was dragged down by my friends' Donkey ego and insecurity.

I believe that cutting ties with negative people is essential to your emotional and mental health. Young or old, Unicorns are susceptible to being lured into the dark. When you aren't absolutely sure of who you are, you're most at risk of being seduced by people who confirm your worst fears for yourself. If you worry that you're useless, you'll surround yourself with lazy people who talk about the futility of reaching for the stars. During my party phase, I thought the people I did drugs with were my friends, but they were self-destructive and, in hindsight, only helped me destroy myself. I wish I'd stayed away, and I urge anyone on the edge of falling into the darker side not to go near them.

Unicorns are magical creatures that shimmer *in the light.* Stay out in the open, under the rainbow, awash in incandescent pixie dust. Just as dark attracts dark, light attracts light. Look for the light that shines in others and for the glow to reflect back on you. The dark is a black hole, a swamp, not the place for Unicorns to thrive and run free.

When I choose friendships, I don't care about people's looks, status, or money. I only care about whether they are generous, kind, joyful, and bright. I look for explorers, dreamers, *laughers.* How do they deal with problems? Can they turn a negative experience into a chance for growth? How do they generate and process their ideas? How do they celebrate a victory? Handle a failure?

IT'S HARD TO BE A DIAMOND IN A RHINESTONE WORLD.

DOLLY PARTON, BRAINY BOMBSHELL

Admit they're wrong? Support me? Do they strive to up their Unicorn quotient every minute of the day? That's someone who will take you higher, a friend worth having.

GREGORY AND ME

I've met dozens of magical people in my life and befriended some world-class artists and creators, legends in their field, who taught me about the creative lifestyle. I had the great good fortune to make a deep Unicorn Connection over many years with Gregory Hines, the legendary tap dancer and hoofer.

Gregory was born with fast feet and started dancing professionally as a little boy. His enthusiasm and passion got him noticed, but it was his kindness, humor, and generosity that made him really stand out. He worked with other Unicorn legends such as Mel Brooks in *History of the World, Part I*, Francis Ford Coppola in *The Cotton Club*, and Mikhail Baryshnikov in *White Nights*. His screen role I love most is in *Waiting to Exhale,* when he tells his built-for-comfort love interest, "I like a woman to have some meat on her bones." He once had his own primetime variety program on CBS called *The Gregory Hines Show*, and he made many cameo appearances on TV, including a recurring role on *Will and Grace.* He shined the brightest on Broadway, winning a Tony for best actor in the role of Jelly Roll Morton in 1992, and he was nominated three more times. The year before he died, he co-hosted the Tony Awards with Queen Unicorn Bernadette Peters. In the dance world, Gregory was a god. Everyone knew him, loved him, and respected him. I, for one, worshiped him for his talent and for his brilliance at making every moment an adventure.

I saw Gregory for the first time on TV when I was a little girl and knew that we were connected in some way, as if our Unicorn energies reached through the television and linked up. I felt like he could see me through the screen. I just knew I'd meet him one day and that there would be a special connection.

Years later, my sister was taking a master class tap seminar at a studio in SoHo, New York, and Gregory was one of the masters. He had a book signing that weekend at a local studio, so I decided to go with Dana and actually meet him. There was a line around the block to get his autograph. We waited for two hours before finally reaching the table where he was sitting. He signed Dana's book and then looked up at me, paused, and said, "Hi."

In the crowded bookstore, with a line of people behind me, Gregory and I locked eyes and just grinned at each other as if we'd met somewhere before. He asked me my name. For me, it was as if he was moving in slow motion, but we had to keep the line moving, so we left.

When we were outside, Dana asked, "What was *that?*" It was an immediate, intense Unicorn Connection, a new, amazing feeling for me. Meeting my hero was everything I thought it would be. Completely exhilarated, Dana and I practically floated down the street. We hadn't gone ten feet, though, before I heard someone calling my name.

It was Gregory. He'd left his own book signing to chase me down. "Can we stay in touch?" he asked. We exchanged numbers. The next day, we had lunch together and started one of the most important, dynamic, and inspired friendships of my life.

One time, Gregory and I were spending some time in Santa Monica and, after dinner, we returned to the hotel where an amazing jazz band was playing in the lobby. As soon as we pushed through the revolving doors and heard the music, we began to dance. Every person in the lobby and the bar stopped what they were doing to watch Gregory, the legendary tapper himself. He could have had a bag over his head and they still would have been transfixed by his dancing. We improvised a number and danced all the way across the lobby toward the elevator. At exactly the right moment, the doors opened. Gregory and I slid into the elevator with perfect timing. We even turned to take a quick bow just as the doors closed and we lifted up into the stratosphere (or was it just the fifth floor?). The entire two-minute improvisation was so perfect, you'd have thought it was painstakingly choreographed or even filmed for a movie. That was Gregory to a T. For him, every moment was a sublime creation. He spread the joy of life to everyone he met. You bet the jazz band stepped up their game when they saw him, and the lucky spectators felt more alive the rest of the day and maybe went to the beach to find a spontaneous adventure of their own.

Maybe Gregory lived so intensely because he knew he didn't have any time to waste.

At fifty-seven, he died of liver cancer. His funeral was star studded. I remember watching all the hoofers from Broadway's *Bring in 'da Noise, Bring in 'da Funk*, Savion Glover, his tap-son, included, leaning over the coffin—crying and dancing as if they were grieving through their feet. It was the most beautiful, powerful, and heartbreaking tribute. Gregory was truly beloved. I was glad that, after two divorces, he'd found love with Negrita Jayde before he died.

He inspired me constantly in the way he lived with abundance, joy, and celebration, a man with the heart of a child. As an artist and a human being, he was light, laughter, originality, knowledge, rhythm, music, and style. Gregory was a King Unicorn who left us way too soon. I miss his magic.

	HIM/HER/THEM	HIM/HER/THEM
YOU	• You share a love for adventure and will be each other's partner in crime. • You'll introduce each other to new worlds and ideas. • Experimental in bed! • You'll push each other to new creative heights. • You might get competitive with each other. • If you or your significant other gets inspired, you might not see each other for a while. • You get in big, dramatic fights. • Things might get *too* intense. • Even though you strive to fight insecurity, jealousy could rear its ugly horn.	• Your significant other will love you madly. You are the magic in his or her life. • You'll always feel like the star in the relationship. • He or she will be reliable. • You can be as unpredictable as you want to be, and he or she will accept it. • Your significant other might get frustrated with your need for privacy. • He or she might feel overwhelmed with your powerful emotions. • You might get frustrated with his or her unwillingness to try new things, in and out of bed. • He or she is predictable.
YOU	• You will love how exciting your significant other is, mentally and sexually. • He or she will push you to challenge yourself. • You like your role as his or her stable, reliable supporter. • You might feel overshadowed, but, if ego doesn't get in the way, you can handle it. • There might be a conflict around socializing. You want to go out more, and he or she wants to stay in. Or vice versa. • Sometimes, you just wish he or she would act normal. • Too much adventure can be exhausting. • His or her eccentricities might embarrass you.	• You two have a comfortable partnership. • You confirm each other's beliefs in the way things should be. • You'll enjoy a satisfying if vanilla sexual relationship. • You cheer each other on. • You'll fight occasionally about things you can't control, like money and in-laws. • Inspiring each other to reach new goals isn't all that important in your day-to-day life. • Together, you focus on practical matters and steer clear of deeper ones. • You don't worry about how other people perceive you as a couple.

UNICORN-DONKEY DATING MATRIX

Should Unicorns date their own kind only? Can a mixed couple of a Donkey and a Unicorn find true love? Of course, because we're all part Unicorn (in some situations) and part Donkey (in others), there are so many possible combinations along the continuum, some that are long-term magical connections and some that flare up and blaze out in a ball of glory and tears.

In the matrix on the previous page, I refer to people who are solidly Unicorn or Donkey, who identify very clearly as one or the other. In each of the four quadrants—Unicorn/Unicorn, Donkey/Unicorn, Donkey/Donkey, and Unicorn/Donkey—I've listed positives and negatives for each pairing. These insights come from real-life experiences of my own or of my close friends.

UNICORN HEARTACHE

One question that comes up often when I speak about Unicorns is, "Do they suffer deeper heartache than Donkeys?"

Not to be glib about love, but I believe Unicorns fall especially hard. When the end of the relationship comes, a Donkey skids on the surface of heartache, but a Unicorn's whole world is shattered. The more sensitive you are, the more you suffer, so, yes, Unicorns have it worse emotionally. But creatively, heartache is fabulous for Unicorns as a source of growth and inspiration. A devastating breakup might be just what they need to take their insight and awareness of self to new glowing-horn heights.

In a painless, idyllic world, a relationship ends cleanly, is followed by a short, reflective period, after which you zoom into another affair that erases the memory of the previous one.

TAKE YOUR
BROKEN HEART,
MAKE IT
INTO ART.

 CARRIE FISHER, THE ORIGINAL BUNHEAD

Sounds boring, doesn't it?

Unicorns are passionate and intense; their relationships (soul matches, not flings) hardly ever fade away gently. All of my relationships have been drawn out, frustrating, and ultimately devastating. My longest lasted for five years during my mid-twenties. I was a Unicorn in training then, magic and creative but still learning to love and respect myself. I wasn't thrilled with my body at the time and questioned my desirability. My father's voice from my teen years—"It only matters how you look!"—still rattled around in my head, and insecurity made me a jealous girlfriend. My demons were in bed with us, and they took up way too much space.

Despite my issues, we were in love and talked about getting engaged.

We broke up in wintertime in New York. I was away teaching at a dance convention for the weekend, and I was so happy finally to come home to my apartment in Chelsea. Usually, when I got home, he was happy to see me. That night, instead of running up to me as I came through the door and wrapping me in his arms, he just stood there. Something was clearly on his mind. We'd had a fight two nights prior on the phone, and he must have still been upset about it.

We talked for a few minutes, and then he said suddenly, "I'm going to go home tonight." He put on his coat and left. The door closed behind him and, when I heard that loud *click*, a premonition flashed before my eyes. *I'll never see him again.*

I got undressed to shower, but that horrible feeling of being abandoned did not let go. I couldn't act like nothing had happened. The man I wanted to marry just left my apartment without even kissing me goodbye. My vision played before my eyes once more. *I'll never see him again.*

I threw on my bathrobe and decided to go find him. He couldn't have gone far in the three minutes since he'd left. I would catch him and demand an explanation. That was the plan, anyway. I opened the door and ran down West 22nd Street, barefoot, in the snow, my robe flapping in the wind, crying and shouting his name, like a deranged woman. I circled the block, but he was nowhere to be found. My feet were blue and my teeth started chattering, so I went back home, defeated and miserable.

True to my vision, I never saw him again.

He was a creative genius, a composer, who wrote beautiful, haunting music. But he wasn't brave or kind. He pretended to be compassionate, but the cruel truth came out that night, and I suffered for it.

We never had the post-breakup talk or run-in at a party. After an intense, passionate five years together, he walked out and never communicated with me again. It just . . . stopped. He left me with a gaping hole in my chest for months. The pain was real, the worst, physical, full-body ache that felt like the muscle soreness of a high fever. There is nothing like a broken heart to make you dread waking up in the morning. Many of my dance company's pieces were set to his music, so I had to listen to it during rehearsals over and over again. Which meant agony over and over again.

To this day, I have no idea what happened. He refused to explain himself, despite my giving him many opportunities to do so. I admit to some weak moments of going to his apartment and buzzing him, calling him at home and work a dozen times a day. Dignity? I was a mess! I couldn't have cared less about how it all looked and what my desperation was doing to me. Not having closure only prolonged my pain.

Needless to say, I'm over it now. It's been twenty years! I look back at that night, running and crying in the snow, and laugh at how insane I must have looked and how, if I were in his shoes (any shoes), I might've ducked into an alley to avoid dealing with me, too. Still, after five years together, he could have given me an explanation, but he chose to be a coward.

When I talk about making choices that push your Unicorn quotient toward diamond-studded glory, it includes how you handle yourself when you'd really rather hide from uncomfortable emotions. Being in a relationship is a responsibility two people share equally, and you can both push your Unicorn Meter in the right direction with honesty, compassion, and bravery, Unicorn qualities that the world needs more of.

If you are wronged by the callousness of an ex, don't waste time blaming yourself or that person. Do what you can for yourself, which means facing the pain head-on and allowing it to sink all the way to your bones so that it will pass through you more quickly. Eventually, I turned to work for healing, and it worked. People may disappoint you or leave, but the fire inside, your creativity and passion, will never go out. When I need to be consoled, I focus on my work, meditate, exercise, and hang out on my couch with my bulldog, Lily, perhaps not in that order.

If I had a daughter, I'd tell her, "Please don't make the mistake I did of putting your happiness and sanity in someone else's hands." Love can fill your heart with joy, but you have to rely on yourself for happiness by truly loving yourself first. When romance fails, your career will be there for you. Of course, creative work can be just as frustrating and your heart can break over

I'M AFRAID I HAVE VERY FEW
FRIENDS AND I THINK THAT ALL
OF THE FRIENDS I HAVE, I CAN
DEPEND ON AND THEY CAN DEPEND
ON ME. SO IF YOU HAVE GOT ME
AS A FRIEND, YOU'VE GOT ME FOR
LIFE. AND I'D DO ANYTHING FOR
THEM, BUT I DON'T REALLY HAVE
ASSOCIATES THAT USE ME OR
ABUSE ME, UNLESS I ASK THEM TO!

ALEXANDER McQUEEN, VISIONARY DESIGNER

disappointments and endings in that realm, too. But at least your creativity is in your control. That fire in your heart is a guiding force, an eternal flame that never goes out.

My amazing life coach, Libby Moore, taught me a technique for self-love: spend a few minutes every morning looking at yourself in the mirror. Look deep into your eyes, and tell yourself how much you love yourself. Call yourself by name, saying, "I love you, _____." The first time I did this, I cried because it was like looking into the eyes of the vulnerable, awkward, lonely child I had been. I highly recommend this exercise.

ARE UNICORNS PARTY ANIMALS?

Many Unicorns, myself included, are loners who prefer a quiet Saturday night home alone to socializing. Other Unicorns are extroverts who seek out and love to shine in the spotlight.

Which are you? It's important to know so you can relieve yourself of the pressure to be someone other than who you are. Society says it's bad or wrong to spend too much time alone, so when Unicorn introverts push themselves to "get out there," they can exhaust themselves and expend their creative energy on conversations that are probably meaningless in the long run (or the short run). Society also dictates that creative minds thrive on solitude and focus, so extroverted Unicorns might think they need to be alone to create but will actually gain energy and be stimulated into inspiration when they are around other people. Remember the question of authenticity: "How am I *not* myself?" One way is how you socialize and the demands you make on yourself that might not fit your unique Unicorn social needs.

QUIZ: ARE YOU AN INTROVERT UNICORN OR AN EXTROVERT UNICORN?

1. A casual friend is throwing a party. You won't know many of the other guests. How do you feel about going?
   a. Excited about the opportunity to meet new people.
   b. Meh. You'll get free wine and food, but making small talk is annoying.
   c. Terrified. Mingling with strangers is like pulling teeth. You'd rather stay home.
2. How do you feel about being alone?
   a. Hate it! After an hour or two by yourself, you get antsy and make calls to meet up with friends.
   b. It's okay. You look forward to solitude, but after a weekend without plans, you start to feel depressed.
   c. Excellent. You can go for days on end with just books and Netflix to keep you company. Sometimes, your scant social needs scare you.
3. If a stranger talks to you while you're in line at the supermarket, what do you do?
   a. Pick up the conversational ball and run with it. Chance stranger conversations make your day, and the good vibes last for hours.
   b. Respond politely. Depending on your mood, random interactions can be fun or irritating.
   c. Respond resentfully. If it weren't for basic civility, you'd ignore the interruption and go back to your own thoughts.
4. How does your personality change depending on whom you're with?

(continued)

a. No change at all. You're always the same, whether you're with friends and family or complete strangers.

b. A bit tailored. You're goofier with people you trust and a bit guarded with strangers until you get a sense of where they're coming from.

c. A lot. If you don't know them, you don't engage. You don't even know how to act naturally with strangers. When you're with close friends and trusted family members, you can relax and be yourself.

5. You're settled in for the evening, and then a friend calls to ask you to come out for a drink. What do you do?

a. Go out! Nothing's happening at home, and who knows what might happen out there? You never pass up a chance to have fun and socialize.

b. It depends. Many factors to consider, like how far you'd have to travel, the weather, your schedule the next day, how rich you feel. If you do go out, you're usually glad you did.

c. Don't even answer the phone. Nothing is going to get you out of the house once your lounge pants are on. If you haven't mentally prepared for an interaction, there is no way you're going to spontaneously throw yourself into one. It's just too jarring.

6. When you need to sort things out or solve a problem, what do you do?

a. Talk it out with someone else. You get to those breakthroughs while discussing things with a sounding board.

    b. A combination of talking to someone you trust and thinking through the problem by yourself.

    c. Contemplate potential outcomes and solutions by yourself.

7. When you're home alone and then a family member or roommate walks in, do you:

    a. Rush to greet the person and chat, leaving the TV or stereo on because you like the background noise.

    b. Call out "hello" and pause what you're doing before spending a few minutes catching up with the person. Maybe you'll crack open a bottle of wine, watch a show, or have some food together. You're just as likely to go back to your room or office and finish what you were doing.

    c. Say "hello" and keep on doing whatever you were doing until you're mentally prepared to deal with another person. Then and only then will you leave your room and interact.

SCORING

Mostly As: You're a Unicorn extrovert.

Mostly Bs: You're a Unicorn ambivert.

Mostly Cs: You're a Unicorn introvert.

Like the Unicorn-Donkey Continuum, your comfort with and enthusiasm for social interaction is on a scale that looks like this:

INTROVERT   AMBIVERT   EXTROVERT

(continued)

Right in the middle are the **Unicorn ambiverts**. Those who see a dichotomy in their lives between their Unicorn and Donkey selves are more likely to fit in this category. If you are an ambivert, you are as comfortable speaking in front of a group of people as you are at home by yourself. You're flexible and can shift from one situation to the next without having to mentally prepare. You can be the life of the party for a while, but then you can step away from the spotlight and enjoy a quiet conversation with just one other person or leave early.

Other people might annoy you at times, but you don't freak out like a trapped rat if you're stuck in a conversation with someone you don't relate to. You make small talk until you figure a way to escape politely. Unlike extroverts, who love to hear the sound of their own voice, or introverts, who often block out other people, you can listen to other people and really hear what they're trying to say. Ambiverts use their flexibility to tailor their behavior to a given situation. For example, say you're at a family reunion. You can decide "Time to shift into extrovert mode." If you have a big deadline, you can just as easily switch into introvert mode and get the job done.

Unicorn ambiverts' social need: balanced. Like your Unicorn-Donkey ratio (sometimes you're one, sometimes you're the other), your ratio of need for face time versus alone time might depend on what you're doing and whom you're with, and you can probably trust your gut instincts to make the decisions for you without too much agonizing. We all have obstacles to increasing our Unicornness, but social balance isn't one of yours. That said, you have cycles and moods. If you find yourself veering to one side for too long, gently nudge yourself back toward the center to avoid social burnout and isolation-related depression.

To the far right are the **Unicorn extroverts**, born socializers. Being with people gives you energy. You're outgoing, engaging, and comfortable being the center of attention. Correction: you're *more* than comfortable with it. You need it, like food and oxygen. You thrive on attention and wither without it. Small talk is as natural as breathing and you can do it with anyone—or anything; a lamppost will do. Parties full of strangers aren't intimidating at all. You plunge right in and make ten new best friends in the first hour because Donkeys and other Unicorns are drawn to your glowing, iridescent light. You get a big ego rush when you charm people, which is one of your Donkeyish traits.

On the downside, fear of missing out plagues you. Because of your Unicorn curiosity and thirst for adventure, it drives you crazy to think that something cool or exciting is happening in the world without you. As a result, you *always* show up for parties and events, even if they're sure to disappoint.

Being alone can be uncomfortable at first, and painful before too long. Solitary confinement is your worst nightmare. Even if you're not actually watching the TV, you like to have it playing in the background just to hear the

(continued)

voices. Unicorn extrovert writer friends type with the TV or music at full blast or in crowded, noisy cafes; I have no idea how they can concentrate, but they tell me they can't create otherwise. To solve a problem, Unicorn extroverts prefer to "talk it through" with someone they respect and trust, and they're not afraid of blurting out ideas that might seem strange in a professional meeting or setting. They have a real advantage in that they work well in groups, which is prized in corporate culture.

I've met a lot of Unicorn extroverts in my career in show biz, and I liked about half of them. In my introverted way, I've observed that good talkers aren't good listeners and being talked at, for an introvert, can feel like being under assault.

Unicorn extroverts' social need: so freaking high. You already know that human connection is your life force, but be warned, Unicorn extroverts: you might figure things out by speaking out loud to others, but you won't learn anything new just listening to yourself talk. Being a Unicorn means breaking out of your safe space and trotting into undiscovered country. For you, that means talking *less,* listening *more,* and forcing yourself to spend *some* time alone—two nights a week—without relying on TV, music, or social media for company. It'll feel twitchy and itchy at first, which is what you're after. See what happens to your mind when you are alone with your thoughts. You won't explode with unspoken words, I promise.

Last, but not least, we have **Unicorn introverts,** a blaze I am a lifelong member of. We aren't necessarily shy—that's a big misconception. We're just quiet and don't feel compelled to be loud, hog attention, or prove how smart we are. Just because you're not dazzling the room with your wit doesn't mean your thoughts aren't clever, relevant, and insightful. As author Susan Cain writes in *Quiet: The Power of Introverts in a World That Can't Stop Talking,* "The loudest person in the room isn't always the smartest." As Unicorns, you draw attention without words—horn on forehead—so you don't need to shout anyway. You would rather not speak unless you have something important to say.

When you're in social situations that require participation, like a dinner party or business meeting, the stress of conversation can be overwhelming. For some Unicorn introverts, just a few minutes of small talk is exhausting, depleting them of creative energy. However, in a small group of trusted friends or one on one with new people, you can be just as charming as any extrovert. It could take a keg of dynamite to get the cat or dog off their lap and to get Unicorn introverts off the couch on a weekend night. Solitude isn't a luxury; it's a necessity. Quiet contemplation nurtures your soul.

Most Unicorn introverts prefer to work their magic behind the scenes. As one who appears in front of the camera and who is in charge of directing other people, I'm an exception. For me to get the job done, I have to be loud and think fast, even though my natural tendency is to be quiet and to take my time, thinking something through

(continued)

and then bringing it to life through dancers' bodies. I'm often forced into draining conversations, small talk, and logistical stuff. Afterward, I have to sit alone for a while to equalize, and my mind just drifts, and I float along with it. If I can't get my zone-out time, I feel disconnected from myself.

Unicorn introverts' social need: really low. You can be your own best friend, but even Unicorn introverts need *some* human connection. Psychological research has proven that daily face-to-face interactions boost longevity and emotional health. Set a quota for the number of connections you need each day, and fill it. Start with three (they can be random conversations with strangers or dinner with a partner). Unicorns need to push their boundaries to learn and grow, so up your socializing quota gradually. You tend to get your best ideas by yourself, but once in a while, an interaction will flip the switch in you. "We can stretch our personalities, but only up to a point," writes *Quiet* author Susan Cain. If you're a Unicorn introvert, you'll never suddenly be the life of the party, but it can't hurt to show up once in a while, just to see what happens.

THE KEY

To find your blaze:

Calibrate your Unicorn-dar. Your horn is like a homing signal that will glow when you're near others of your kind. Use this power to find like-minded free spirits to romp on the Rainbow Path together. But if you love a Unicorn, let them go. Unicorn friendships are about synergy and inspiration, not obligation and guilt trips. People come in and out of your life for a reason, so be present in the relationship while it lasts, and always be grateful for its lessons. But don't forget your alone time to charge your Unicorn batteries.

AS AN ADOLESCENT, I WAS
PAINFULLY SHY, WITHDRAWN.
I DIDN'T REALLY HAVE THE NERVE
TO SING MY SONGS ON STAGE AND
NOBODY ELSE WAS DOING THEM.
I DECIDED TO DO THEM IN
DISGUISE SO THAT I DIDN'T HAVE
TO ACTUALLY GO THROUGH THE
HUMILIATION OF GOING ON STAGE
AND BEING MYSELF. I DESIGNED
CHARACTERS WITH THEIR OWN
COMPLETE PERSONALITIES AND
ENVIRONMENTS. I EVEN PUT THEM
INTO INTERVIEWS WITH ME! IT WAS
A VERY STRANGE THING TO DO.

DAVID BOWIE, CHAMELEON

STEP SIX

FEAR IS YOUR FRIEND

SO FAR, YOU'VE GAINED SELF-RESPECT, LEARNED to own your dark secrets, polished your pure heart, grown a bulletproof hide, and sorted out your social connection needs. The first five steps are like table legs (a table with five legs? Isn't that STRANGE?), giving you a firm, stable foundation to build your magical realm upon.

Step six is next-level Unicorn. You will learn to lean in to fear.

I won't deny that writing a book is outside my comfort zone, and I practice what I preach just by trying. I throw myself into terrifying situations in the hope that I'll push past barriers and learn about myself and the world, and ultimately grow from that. Every time I sit down to write—or go into a studio, or begin a relationship—I'm scared. Venturing into the unknown keeps my art and my heart alive. I made a deal with myself long ago that if I'm not terrified about what comes next, then I'm not evolving as an artist or human. To create, you need to make yourself vulnerable and live in that state of fear of the unknown.

Fear unlocks a deeper level of imagination, or it paralyzes you if you let it. At this point in your Unicorn training, you are ready to embrace your fear of the unknown by saying, "I'm going to do something I've never tried before. I might fall flat on my face—and that's okay!" It's essential for Unicorns to acknowledge their fear to reinforce their ability to push past it.

ANXIETY AND CREATIVITY GO HAND IN HAND

Unicorns are creative people, and an unfortunate side effect of being imaginative and innovative is anxiety. I'm not just saying this: psychological studies have proven that creative types are more likely to be anxious and to struggle with symptoms of an anxiety disorder, such as racing thoughts that spiral out of control and obsessiveness. The anxious mind is so imaginative that it can come up with all kinds of crazy scenarios—some that are frightful—and just having the mental image of what can go wrong can fill you with dread. Donkeys' minds don't "go there" as readily, so they don't wrestle and fret as much with what could go horribly wrong.

For some people, anxiety is not just in their mind, it's in their *brain*. Scientists have found that people who have an anxiety disorder—suffering from panic attacks and persistent ruminations—have brains that are wired differently, and, here's the kicker, there is a link between this kind of wiring and creative genius.

- **Charles Darwin**, the English scientist who came up with the idea of evolution and completely changed the way we think about biology and nature, was a famous neurotic who was so crippled by panic attacks, he would spontaneously throw up when stressed out.

- **Isaac Newton**, the American who discovered gravity, was a well-known worrier who fretted about his theories.
- **Nikola Tesla**, the Serbian-born electrical engineer who invented an alternating current electric motor and worked with X-rays and early robotics, was so neurotic, obsessive, and prone to panic attacks that he became the model for the "mad scientist" stereotype.
- **Sigmund Freud**, the Austrian psychologist, had such crippling social anxiety he was basically a hermit for the last years of his life.

All were innovators. All of them changed how we think of ourselves and the world. And all of them were anxious.

Being a nervous person does make life harder, but I hope it helps just to know that a fretful brain comes with a fresh, original take on the world.

THE UNCOMFORTABLE EDGE

The key to creativity for *everyone* (not just those with severe anxiety) is being uncomfortable and vulnerable and using that tension and uncertainty as inspiration. None of us has a clue about or have even touched the depth and vastness of our potential, but if you go into a project afraid and unsure and emerge the better for it, you will learn that limits exist only in the mind. You'll get closer to your optimal self.

When you're at the beginning of something new—a project, a job, a relationship, anything—and it feels like you're about to step off a cliff into a black hole, you are sliding the meter toward diamond-studded Unicorn mode. Feeling scared is how you push past boundaries, break pavement, and move into new territory.

On the other hand, if you start something new and it feels like slipping into a warm bath, you are nudging yourself toward cardboard-cutout Donkey-hood. Feeling safe, snug, and secure is a cozy trap that locks you into the status quo, which equals basicness. Copying yourself feels good, especially to the ego. You see it in the careers of people who make the same movie over and over again or write the same book or song in slightly different variations over the years. Being safe doesn't help you discover what you're capable of; making copies over and over is not being an artist or a creative human being. It's called being a robot.

> FEELING SAFE, SNUG, AND SECURE IS A COZY TRAP THAT LOCKS YOU INTO THE STATUS QUO, WHICH EQUALS BASICNESS.

No one likes feeling uncomfortable, but we need to welcome it to see what's on the other side. Creativity is about invention, reinvention, subversion, and danger. To be an original, an evolved Unicorn, you have to embrace discomfort, even if it causes you pain in the midst of the creative process. When I find myself on the verge of a major self-doubt meltdown, I tell myself, "Hang in there. This is where it gets good." And, usually, you need to push through barriers to have a real breakthrough.

You have to actively seek out the uncomfortable edge and force your feet to walk up to it. Your primal instinct will try to steer you away from danger and toward the safe and comfortable. Override the innate fight-or-flight reflex when you encounter something that makes you nervous, and unleash the Unicorn hunger that feeds on taking risks and trying new things. And then, you have to muster all of your courage and jump off that edge into the unknown.

WHAT ARE YOU AFRAID OF?

When I'm working with students or dancers who seem to be holding back, I ask a simple question that cuts to the heart of the matter: "What are you afraid of?"

Often, they don't give me an honest answer because they're AFRAID to share their truth with me—or they're terrified of the truth itself and the truth of being judged. Franklin D. Roosevelt once said, "You have nothing to fear but fear itself." I'll edit that for Unicorns: "You have nothing to fear *from the truth* itself." Fear controls you only when you don't or can't acknowledge what it is and where it comes from, which brings me right back to where I started. What *exactly* is holding you back? What fear is blocking you from reaching your full Unicorn potential?

Just by identifying and naming your fear, you take the first step to diminishing it.

All internal fears—the kind that originate inside you—derive from ego and insecurity, the two big pernicious Donkey traits. Donkeys' egos want to stay intact, and scary situations where Donkeys might fail threaten their sense of self. If there's any chance Donkeys might be ridiculed or judged harshly for trying something new or expressing their vulnerability, they won't do it, whatever "it" is, from asking someone out to wearing quirky clothes, singing or acting on stage, dancing like no one is watching, or reading poetry aloud. They only do what they already know they do well to feel safe and secure. Even the *idea* of doing something different triggers insecurity that has them running for a safe space.

External fears—the kind that originate outside you, such as tigers, hurricanes, strange noises in the dark—are legit and valid. When I talk about befriending fear, I mean your internal ones. Putting yourself in harm's way by being reckless and stupid with external fears does not increase your freedom and authenticity. If anything, it makes you a slave to an unhealthy, self-destructive adrenaline addiction. Not cool, and not Unicorn.

Carrie Fisher, actor/author/alien princess, struggled with mental illness and addiction, but she didn't let her problems stop her from taking risks and pursuing her goals. She wrote in her memoir *Wishful Drinking*, "Stay afraid, but do it anyway. What's important is the action. You don't have to wait to be confident. Just do it and eventually the confidence will follow."

When you come face to face with your fears, what do they look and sound like? What thoughts or sentences do you use to explain your fear?

"**I can't do it!**" or "**It can't be done.**" These two thoughts relate to **fear of failure**, which tops the list for irrational self-sabotage. No one can know if they can or can't do something until they put all of their power and energy into succeeding at it first. And even then, every so-called failure gets you one step closer to success. Thomas Edison, when asked about his failed attempts to make an incandescent light bulb, said, "I have not failed seven hundred times. I have not failed once. I have succeeded in proving that

YOUR TIME IS LIMITED,

SO DON'T WASTE IT LIVING

SOMEONE ELSE'S LIFE.

DON'T LET THE NOISE OF

OTHERS' OPINIONS DROWN

OUT YOUR OWN INNER VOICE.

 STEVE JOBS, THE MAN WHO CHANGED IT ALL

those seven hundred ways will not work. When I have eliminated the ways that will not work, I will find the way that will work." If Edison gave up after a hundred, or four hundred, or seven hundred tries, you might be reading this book by candlelight.

"No one will like me anyway" or **"If I put it all out there, they'll laugh at me."** A cousin of fear of failure is the **fear of rejection.** You don't want to look like an idiot or an asshole, so you don't bother trying. This fear is a sin of vanity. You're so afraid of how you'll look and what people will think that you don't allow yourself to experiment and evolve as a human being or a creative force. Every single time you know you might look ridiculous in public but you choose to go for it anyway nudges your Unicorn quotient in the right direction. Go ahead and sing karaoke. Wear a crazy Halloween costume. Make a toast at your friend's wedding. Overcoming small fears leads to crushing the biggies.

"Even if it does go my way, what the hell do I do then?" or **"If I succeed, I might not like what happens as a result."** Believe it or not, **fear of success** is just as common, I think, as fear of failure. One tells you you can't do something, and the flip side is that you can do something but that you won't be able to cope with what comes next, in other words, **fear of the unknown.** Preventing growth because you're comfortable in the familiar is an excellent way to Krazy Glue a Donkey disguise on your back. The Unicorn way is to feel frightened but to jump into the unknown anyway.

HOLY SHIT!

By writing this book, I'm right back at that place of saying, "Holy shit. Where do I start? How do I do this?" All of a sudden, I'm at the foot of a mountain, looking up and wondering how I'm going to climb that. I don't even know the first thing about being an author. It's a beautiful feeling. It's a horrible feeling. As an artist, it's where we need to live, and I'll always seek it out. Not that I go out looking to stand in the middle of the road to get hit by a truck— figuratively, of course; I'm actually careful lately about my health and wellness—but if I'm careful creatively, I don't feel fully alive.

Every single time I enter a studio, teach a class, choreograph a show, or write a *book*, I'm compelled to take risks. Saying "yes" is the same as saying "holy shit!" for me. As a result, I'm choosey about what I sign on to do. I make a deal with myself as an artist that I am going to take it as far as I can go and push myself as far as I can. As a creator, if I'm not uncomfortable, it's not happening. Every artist needs that feeling of being vulnerable and scared. You don't have to completely freak yourself out! But make your heart beat faster every day and get excited about the unknown.

THE KEY

To make friends with fear:

Don't think too hard about why you're afraid, because you might talk yourself out of the uncomfortable zone (where genius lives). But have at least a basic understanding of what you're really frightened of, be it fear of failure, success, uncertainty, or rejection, and jump! Fear is like an imaginary friend that is invisible and standing right next to you. Take it by the hand, and leap into the unknown, feet first!

IF WE BELIEVE IN MAGIC,

WE'LL LIVE A MAGICAL LIFE.

IF WE BELIEVE OUR LIFE IS

DEFINED BY NARROW LIMITS,

WE'VE SUDDENLY MADE

THOSE BELIEFS REAL.

 TONY ROBBINS, GURU

STEP SEVEN

LEAP
OF FAITH

IF YOU CAN'T MAKE YOURSELF JUMP INTO THE
unknown using mental strategies, you will absolutely be able to do
it by adding one more important ingredient to the mix: faith!

Unicorns are magical creatures, and there are a lot of other
ones out there, too. You might as well accept and acknowledge that
powerful, positive forces you can't see can help you. If you believe
in fairies and pixies, God, a universal spirit, an electric current
that connects all living things, great. I don't care what your belief system is, as long as you believe in *something* and it's positive.

With faith—first and foremost, in yourself—you can overcome
fear and gain a little extra bit of gratitude and confidence to roll
with life's inevitable ups and downs. You are free to fly, and the
universe wants you to explore its wonders, but you have to take
that first step on your own and believe.

MAGIC IS REAL

One of the visionary artists I've worked with, Italian director
Franco Dragone, the genius behind Cirque du Soleil, taught me

how to catch precious glimpses of magic in everyday life. I met him in 2002, when he was the director of Céline Dion's Las Vegas spectacular "A New Day." My agent called and said I was offered the position as choreographer for this massive show. I didn't hesitate on the uncomfortable edge about working on a project that was bigger and more complex than anything I'd ever done before. I didn't overthink it, I just packed up my New York apartment on that moment's notice and moved to Belgium to work with him.

I arrived in La Louvier and met the mysterious Mr. Dragone for the first time in a dark black box theater, where we began the creative process for the show. I was asked to sit in a chair diagonally behind him to observe the proceedings.

On the God mic, Franco said, "*Lumiere!*" Lights!

Suddenly, the theater lights went up and sixty dancers appeared center stage, as if from thin air. It was a magical start to a beautiful year. During my six months in Belgium and six months in Las Vegas with Franco, he showed me again and again that wonder is always there to be discovered. Be on a constant lookout for beauty, color, texture. Don't just sleepwalk through the day. Notice a beam of light gleaming in the window, the bend of a flower in the breeze, the poetry of existence.

It was creative heaven to work with him. We sparred occasionally, but it only spurred us on and fueled our creative energy. How he saw the world was an education in and of itself. The smallest thing inspired him; just one movement would make him halt a rehearsal and yell, "Everyone! Stop what you're doing and look at this!" and then he'd make the entire cast learn the gesture. He told me, "If you don't find a moment of inspiration in every twenty-four hours, you have lost an entire day of your life."

We all have the capacity to find small inspiring moments every day. It's just that we get bogged down by expectations and obligations and miss the sparks of inspiration flying all around us. Training yourself to look, to scan, to search for magic is like peeling back a cloudy layer in your mind. When the layer is gone, you're open to see the pixie dust swirling around you at all times. You can delve into the world of dreams. Franco saw the world with the eyes of a child, constantly searching for flames of imagination to light up inside himself and all around.

It's crucial for an artist to have that kind of wonder, curiosity, and openness. I adopted his perspective and have been inspired by it ever since. He changed me as an artist and a human. When you take the film off your eyes and look at something in a different way, you can find the art, magic, and inspiration in almost anything.

MAGIC IS EVERYWHERE

I have a writer friend named Violet. She's a bit of a workaholic, and I tell her all the time to step away from the computer for some fresh air and sunshine. "I know, I know," she says, and goes back to work. Then one day, she reached a point of pure exhaustion and couldn't write another word. Her wrists hurt from typing, and her eyes ached from staring at the screen, so she had to take a break and went out to her roof deck.

She sat down on a chair and let herself drift. Usually, her mind stayed focused on whatever she was working on, so this was a rare moment of mental freedom. Her mind turned to thoughts of a dear friend, someone who'd passed tragically years ago. Ordinarily, when his face popped up in her mind, she pushed it away because remembering was too painful. But, that day, fatigue made it impossible to block the thoughts, and memories filled her head.

Then, out of the corner of her eye, she noticed sudden movement. A hummingbird flew directly at her and hovered for a few seconds over the red lantana flowers in the pot right next to her chair. The bird was a mere five inches from her face. It seemed to look at her for a fraction of a second, and then it zoomed away, and was gone.

How often do hummingbirds appear out of nowhere, in October, on a rooftop in Brooklyn?

Violet was blown away by the magic of the moment. She wasn't going to say that the hummingbird was a message of love sent by her deceased friend, but she did say, "It was such a one-in-a-million moment. That I went outside at that time, that I wasn't distracted by a book or my phone, that I noticed the bird, that it noticed me, how we connected, almost like in slow motion, before it disappeared? Those three seconds were a gift. The purest, greatest gift I'd received in a long, long time." She thinks about that moment, and her beloved friend, often these days with joy.

Everyday magic is a gift, and it's there for the taking whenever you open yourself to receive. It's in the sweep of clouds, the wisdom of bells, the dance of butterflies, cats' eyes, babies' skin, the scent of fresh-cut lemon. Open your senses to it, and you'll be flooded with delicious wonder.

UNICORN SPEAK

J. K. Rowling, author of the Harry Potter novels, a woman who knows a bit about magic, once wrote (in the character of Albus Dumbledore), "*Words* are, in my not-so-humble opinion, our most inexhaustible source of *magic*. Capable of both inflicting injury, and remedying it."

In my always-humble opinion, there's nothing like "I'm sorry" to cure hurt feelings and "Thank you" to spread happiness.

My magic words are positive variations of "I declare." You've heard people on the witness stand in legal dramas say, "I state for the record that . . ." They are making a declaration that what they are about to say is the truth, the whole truth, and nothing but the truth in a court of law. But what about the laws of the universe? When you say, "I state for the record that I'm awesome, capable, or ready," you are making an official declaration of truth.

What you speak comes to life. When you vocalize your dreams and goals and declare them under the sun, moon, and stars, you invite them to manifest as your reality. I know this is hard to believe, but positive thought and speech can change your mood and your mind. Unless you give voice to your desires, you can't make them come true.

I start each day by saying, "I am so beautiful and gorgeous, and I celebrate myself. New doors will open. Boundless blessings are coming my way." To go for the gold, speak out every single thing you want in your life each morning. Making a simple declaration of any goal—"I will get the job" or "I can run a marathon"—is where the journey to success and fulfillment begins. If you're not used to the language of positivity, you have to train yourself for a while before it feels natural. You are not bragging or lying! You are using gratitude and optimism to turn the tide, by an inch or a mile, in your direction.

"I AM." Well, who are you? What makes you? Love originates within. Know yourself to love yourself, and then you can bring that magic to others. (FYI: "I am" is also an anagram of Mia. My name reminds me to be true to myself.) If you're not sure how to finish the sentence, start with general positivity, like, "I am *awesome*," "I am *a Unicorn*," "I am *grateful for being alive and having the courage to figure myself out and dig deeper*."

"I CAN." Remember that little train? He said, "I think I can" get up that hill, and he did. You already know that the hill is a metaphor for any daunting task or challenge. When I have to chug up a mountain, I say, "I can." I don't bother with the "I think" part, because that takes away from the declarative power of two solid syllables: I. CAN. Say it again and again, until you get to say, "I *fucking* did it!"

"I BELIEVE." Believing is a warm-up to manifesting. You have to have faith in your ideas before you make them real. Unless you believe in something—be it a hummingbird's message, a laughing pixie, intuition, love, yourself—your Rainbow Path will look like a parking lot.

"WHY NOT?" Or the slightly profane alternative "Why the fuck not?" Consider the wise words of Unicorn Mark Twain, one of America's greatest storytellers, who said, "Twenty years from now, you will be more disappointed by the things you didn't do than by the ones you did, so throw off the bowlines. Sail away from the safe harbor. Catch the trade winds in your sails. Explore. Dream. Discover." To put it less eloquently, *just fucking do it.* Why not? If nothing more, you'll have a great tale to tell and an experience that adds to your life story.

DONKEY SPEAK

Unicorns often have to deal with a lot of negativity early in life, and they wind up swallowing the taunts and criticisms of hostile Donkeys. Some of the negativity gets under our skin and stays there. Whether we know it consciously or not, we're all susceptible to what I call "knee-jerk negativity." You don't even hear the self-trashing voice in your head. It's the echo of a critical parent, a teacher, a mean girl from junior high, your first love who dumped you, the boss who fired you. Those negative influencers get their hooks in you, and they don't want to let go. The way to shake them out of your head is to tune in to knee-jerk negativity when it crops up and shut that shit *down*. In other words, cancel the noise.

You define who you are. The negative voices from the past can be silenced with the Unicorn magic words listed above and by cutting off any statement or thought that starts with defeatist Donkey language, like the following:

"I SHOULD." I should lose weight. I should quit smoking. I should write my novel. I should quit my soul-sucking dead-end job. All of those statements might be true. But using "I should" gives you permission not to do the thing you want to do. The unspoken second half of the sentence is ". . . but I won't." Replace "I should" with "I can." That way, when you're ready to take action, you'll know it's in your power to make the changes you wish for.

"I HAVE TO." This is the mirror opposite of "I should." "I should" lets you off the hook, but "I have to" puts you on it. When I hear "I have to," it makes me think of an authority figure, a parent or a teacher, coming down hard on me. "You have to . . . change, be better, do things my way, be someone other than who you are." Train your brain to get guilt-bringer, pressure-cooker, stress-maker, creativity-killer "I have to" out of your mind, and replace it with "I choose to . . . work hard, do my best, be healthy, etc."

"I CAN'T." If you think and speak in the negative, that's what you get. As soon as you say, "I can't," you have already failed. You are giving up before you try. Granted, there are times when you are not capable—yet—of accomplishing a major goal. So, instead of saying, "I can't do it!" and giving in to frustration, adjust the language to stay optimistic and positive with "I can, and I will."

"I NEED." Unless you are starving and naked on the street, whining about all the things you need that you don't have is like asking the universe to kick you in the teeth. Be grateful for what you already have, Unicorns, starting with your magic, uniqueness, and your glowing, glorious horn.

"WHY ME?" You didn't get exactly what you wanted and can't believe that the universe threw you a curveball? I can smell the entitlement from here. Unicorns don't do self-pity. They know that life doesn't hand us the gold every time. Sometimes, you get a sock full of coal. Celebrate the coal, and know that in time, it'll turn into diamonds.

GOD AND ME

I was raised Catholic and went to Catholic school. My mom and dad eventually became born-again Christians. They gave me a foundation as a believer, but what really locked in my faith was witnessing miracles.

Because of my deformity at a young age, I would take a step and fall down. Not only were my hips turned in, one foot was larger than the other and I had to wear special shoes. More than anything, I wanted to be a ballet dancer, but because of my feet, I couldn't go en pointe without it being very dangerous.

At our studio, we had weekly prayer meetings. At one of those Sunday gatherings when I was nine, a man none of us had ever seen before showed up. He zeroed in on me, walked right over to where I was sitting, and asked, "Can I pray for you?" It should have felt awkward, but it didn't.

The stranger who knew nothing about me, got on his knees and said, "You will dance before kings and queens." Then he reached for my feet, held them, closed his eyes, and started praying. Immediately, my feet heated up. The others gathered around us praying, and, as we all watched, my smaller foot grew and became normal right before our eyes. Everyone gasped, speaking in tongues and saying, "Praise the Lord!" The heat subsided after a few minutes, and the man released my suddenly completely normal feet.

This really happened. I wish I had a video, but smartphones didn't exist back then. My sister was there, and she remembers it as clearly as I do. Over the next couple of days, I was fitted for pointe shoes, and only then did I realize the impact of what had happened. The stranger never came back to the prayer meetings. He'd vanished. No one saw him ever again, and believe me, we looked. I'm convinced he was an angel sent by God to heal me in order to fulfill my destiny in the dance world.

As I've gotten older, I've questioned some aspects of religion in general, but never my wholehearted faith in God. I don't have all the answers about what's out there, and I probably never will, but

I'm a seeker of truth and a believer in spirituality. It's my foundation and a major part of my life every day. We are made up of mostly spirit living in an Earth suit, which was given to us so that we could walk the planet as physical human beings. We have to tend to that part of who we are or we'll never feel fully alive.

Prince was also a strong believer. He once said in an interview for MTV, "I believe in God. I believe in one God. I just want people to know that I'm very sincere in my beliefs. I pray every night, and I don't ask for much. I just say 'thank you.'" Prince and I had many intense conversations about faith, not always agreeing. We can't know what waits for us until we're on the other side, but I am just as sincere as Prince in my belief that I walk with God. No matter how alone I feel, I'm not lost or afraid because I have God on my side, at my side, and inside my heart, and he's holding my hand always. If I take a moment to check in, I feel the warmth.

My faith ignites the fire within. I'm always surrounded by the joy, peace, and clarity. It's like a giant invisible pillow around me, protecting and comforting me. Part of my faith is believing that something greater surrounds me and that I'm living the life I know God intended for me. Was I supposed to get married and have children? Probably not, because I haven't yet. I *was* supposed to teach, heal, and affect the world through my artistry. I know that's why I'm here, and that sense of purpose gives me the courage to live in the uncomfortable uncertainty of a creative life, to jump into the void without any idea where or how I'm going to land. It could be in a tree or on a cloud or on a raft in the ocean. The mystery makes life exciting. I do know that, wherever I land, I'll always land on my feet. My faith that things will always work out, that "this too shall pass," has allowed me to take crazy risks that I can't imagine having taken otherwise.

During the times of my life when I was at my lowest, I've felt more powerful and beautiful because of my faith in God. I'm at my optimal best as a human being when I'm walking and talking with that energy. It allows me to get out of the driver's seat and into the passenger seat, which is not always so easy. Instead of worrying about it, I surrender and follow my intuition and instincts. Somehow, faith takes me where I'm supposed to be. It can be a literal place or just a state of mind.

FINDING MY NEVERLAND

I took a huge leap of faith to work on *Finding Neverland*, a show about Unicorns and magical creatures, about love and faith and pixie dust.

Back in 2014, I was living in Los Angeles, post–*So You Think You Can Dance* and between jobs and unsure what my next big project was going to be. And then I got a call from a movie/stage producer, who asked if I was interested in his upcoming Broadway show based on the Johnny Depp movie about J. M. Barrie's conceiving and writing of the play *Peter Pan*.

I made the decision to sell my house in Los Angeles to move to far more expensive New York. If *Neverland* wasn't a hit, I'd be in dire straits, but I took the risk, knowing that I was put here to push the envelope in life and work, so I did (and so I am).

A week later, I went to the reading of the script in New York with the cast and director Diane Paulus. I sat in the back and just listened. It was beautiful, poignant, heartbreaking, and uplifting, about love and friendship and the power of magic. By the end, I was a mess, absolutely destroyed, sobbing. I realized that everything in my life, every frustration, heartache, happiness, and revelation, had brought me to this project and this moment.

Finding Neverland, at its core, is the story of a Unicorn, a misunderstood oddball artist. As the play opens, the Unicorn is stuck creatively and can't figure out how to take the next step. Then he meets a kid, a Unicorn in training, who is having a very tough life. The two Unicorns form a blaze of their own, and their friendship transforms both of their lives for the better and gives birth to the greatest gift of all, a story we all grew up loving, a story about retaining the wonder of a child and believing in magic.

It was magic itself.

After I recovered from crying at the reading, I immediately started to conceive the movement of the show. It was all about lift and flight, how magic thoughts and pixie dust allow you to fly. It's no wonder so many adults (Donkeys) are stuck on the ground. They weight themselves down with fears and insecurities, but we are all born to fly. Yes, life does come with heavy burdens. But if we can keep the necessary tedious stuff in life to a minimum, we can fly forever, soar through the hard times with pixie dust and giggles. Every single thing my heart needed was right there inside of this show.

I was exactly where I was supposed to be when I signed on to *Neverland*, and the story has inspired me to reach a new level in my artistry. I feel like the universe literally said, "Here you go, Mia. You've done well, and I'm proud of you. Here's a gift."

Finding Neverland is the gift that keeps giving. During its Broadway run, I was reminded of the importance of holding on to a child's magical spirit as we each turn into musty old adults. Unicorns like J. M. Barrie exist in the real world, staying true to their strangeness and contributing something of beauty that's lightened hearts and brightened souls for generations.

We need more Barries! More Bowies! More Unicorns!

THE KEY

To see magic:

Believe in what you can't see. Trust in the cosmic force, or God, or whatever you like. The universe always has your back. Open your mind and peel your eyes for wonders. Miracles do happen.

IF I KNEW WHERE THE GOOD SONGS CAME FROM, I'D GO THERE MORE OFTEN.

LEONARD COHEN, EMOTIONAL EXPLORER

STEP EIGHT

SHIFT
THE
UNIVERSE

SHIFTING THE UNIVERSE WITH ORIGINALITY IS the ultimate goal of an ambitious Unicorn. It's been my primary motivation. But I, and any other Unicorns, can't begin to make great art or live a rich, creative life unless we fill our souls constantly with beauty and wisdom. The quest for inspiration and growth is a major part of every Unicorn's daily life.

To shift the universe, explore the one between your ears. Curiosity is essential. What strange thoughts and oddities send you falling down a rabbit hole? What intrigues you? Learning doesn't end when you graduate. It's a lifelong passion and journey. A universe of knowledge and ideas is out there, just waiting to be discovered, so put down your phone and find a fountain of inspiration that calls to you and only you. What makes your horn glow is not necessarily what makes someone else's light up. This chapter is a gold mine of tricks and triggers from other Unicorns about starting your search for inspiration.

LOOK AROUND

I know some people are inspired by joy and happiness, but I've been inspired by injustice and heartache to create art that can take the pain away. Art is the antidote. In a dance, I set the intension of transforming ugliness into beauty, sadness into relief. One of my Emmy-winning routines on *So You Think You Can Dance* was about addiction, inspired by the call I received about Michael Jackson's death. Simultaneously, I was walking down Hollywood Boulevard and noticed some kids, obvious addicts, living on the street in cardboard shelters. The sight was so disturbing that I felt a need to create a dance of healing for addicts everywhere.

Personally, the only real addictions I have problems with are cigarettes, carbs, and sugar. (Fortunately, I kicked cigarettes, but I still struggle with carbs and sugar.) Seeing those street kids set off something in me that refused to be ignored. When I tap into concepts, I try to dig down and really understand what the life of a junkie must be like. I started moving and unspooling, a process that feels like leaving myself and going into a creative zone without consciousness or presence. I don't remember the specifics about anything I do, but when I revisit at a later time, I look at the work and say, "Whoa. Where'd that come from?" The flow state is most intense when I'm using myself as an instrument and open vessel.

I found myself saying to the dancers, "This is a very important piece and is much larger than us." I pushed one of the dancers the whole time. She was so used to being celebrated as a beautiful, graceful, and sexy dancer. Safe, pretty, and perfect was where she preferred to live. I required her to be ugly in her movement, and going outside her comfort zone frightened her. I forcibly pushed her out of safety, which created frustration and tears. But she fought through it and brought about a major breakthrough in her artistry. The feedback on this dance was bigger than I could have expected. I received thousands of emails from addicts and their loved ones, saying that my piece touched them and helped in some small way.

Another *So You Think You Can Dance* piece I'm proud of was inspired by my father's death. I choreographed a dance about meeting him again in heaven. What would happen, after years apart, when we reconnected? Would we run toward each other, or just wave? The piece was playful, full of laughter, a utopia of love, a celebration of a reunion in heaven—but it was agony to create. In the studio during rehearsals, I couldn't speak my directions and had to write them down because as soon as I opened my mouth, the floodgates let loose. By creating that dance, I was able to mourn my father's death and heal myself in some way. And when the dance premiered on *So You Think You Can Dance*, it was one of my biggest successes because of its honesty and optimism. It spoke to the question we all have about a love lost through death: Will we ever see or meet that person again? I believe that we do.

True stories of the triumph of the human spirit always inspire me. I love documentary films about what people have endured. Otherwise, I turn to music, museums, galleries, fashion, shoes, food, wine, and travel to open doors of creativity for me. Any creative person needs a daily dose of brilliance. If you look, you will find it. Inspiration is all around us, all the time.

ASK QUESTIONS

Unicorn Neil Gaiman, author of *American Gods*, blogged about how he answers the common fan question "Where do you get your ideas?"

"You get ideas from daydreaming," he writes. "You get ideas from being bored. You get ideas all the time. The only difference between writers and other people is we notice when we're doing it."

Unicorns are hyperaware of the working of their minds and are on a constant hunt for ideas. To grab one from the ether, Gaiman suggests asking yourself questions, like, **What if?** . . . "What if you woke up with wings?" he writes. "What if your sister turned into a mouse? What if you all found out that your teacher was planning to eat one of you at the end of term—but you didn't know who?"

Or, **If only** . . . "If only real life was like it is in Hollywood musicals," he writes. "If only I could shrink myself small as a button. If only a ghost would do my homework."

I wonder . . .

If this goes on . . .

Wouldn't it be interesting if . . .

As Gaiman says, "Those questions, and others like them, and the questions they, in their turn, pose ('Well, if cats used to rule the world, why don't they anymore? And how do they feel about that?') are one of the places ideas come from. An idea doesn't have to be a plot notion, just a place to begin creating."

Ideas might flow from a person (could that man be an alien?) or a place (is that telephone booth a portal?), an image (a Rainbow Forest populated by Unicorns?) or by putting two seemingly unrelated things together. His example: "If a person bitten by a werewolf turns into a wolf, what would happen if a goldfish was bitten by a werewolf? What would happen if a chair was bitten by a werewolf?"

The one-plus-one-equals-infinity concept is a favorite of chefs (Asian hotdogs, kosher Mexican, etc.) and fashion designers (delicate Victorian lace on a leather motorcycle jacket). No matter what triggers a flood of ideas, the task at hand is to create something original. I make sure I always ask two final questions: "Am I copying someone else?" and "Am I copying myself?" If so, it's back to the drawing board.

BE A FAN

You want to be a movie director? Then you better watch a lot of movies. Quentin Tarantino once said, "When people ask me if I went to film school, I tell them, 'No, I went to films.'"

- Writers read.
- Musicians go to concerts.
- Artists visit museums.
- Dancers attend performances.
- Chefs go to restaurants.

Look for inspiration across all disciplines. Writers need to go to concerts *and* museums too. Musicians can look at fashion, food, and art to feed their hungry souls. I don't go to a museum or a concert with the single purpose of getting my next big idea, but if one presents itself, fabulous. If not, you've had a fun afternoon and learned something. Win-win-win.

Hardly any big ideas appear fully formed in your head. You might get a piece of one that your brain will put together with other pieces when you're not paying attention, and slowly, the big picture comes into focus.

Unicorn filmmaker David Lynch (*Blue Velvet, Eraserhead*) compared his creative process to fishing for interviewer Paul Holdengräber in a New York Public Library event. "An idea comes, and you see it, and you hear it, and you know it . . . like on a TV in your mind. We don't do anything without an idea, so they're beautiful gifts. And I always say, your desiring an idea is like a bait on a hook—you can pull them in," he said. "And if you catch an idea that you love, that's a beautiful, beautiful day. And you write that idea down so you won't forget it. And that idea that you caught might just be a fragment of the whole—whatever it is you're working on—but now you have even more bait. Thinking about that small fragment—that little fish—will bring in more, and they'll come in and they'll hook on. And more and more come in, and pretty soon you might have a script—or a chair, or a painting, or an idea for a painting."

For the most part, I definitely go fishing for ideas by viewing art in all forms as a fan and a consumer, not only as a creator. I'm blown away by inventiveness, originality, and genius. Taking in art and beholding other people's astonishing creativity make me strive to raise my own game. When you walk among giants, you tend to look up.

DIVE INTO THE COOL

Some people say that substances help them be creative. I admit to smoking some pot earlier on in my creative life, and I called it

I THINK AN ARTIST'S ONLY RESPONSIBILITY IS TO CHASE THEIR INSPIRATION AND TO FALL IN LOVE. IF IT HAPPENS TO MAKE THE WORLD A BETTER PLACE, THAT'S GREAT, BUT IF YOU'RE TRYING TO DO THAT CONSCIOUSLY, IT FEELS LIKE HOMEWORK. WE CAN SMELL WHEN AN ARTIST IS DOING SOMETHING OUT OF OBLIGATION VERSUS "SOMETHING IN ME DEMANDS THAT I WRITE THIS."

LIN-MANUEL MIRANDA, ACTOR, WRITER, SINGER, INNOVATOR, *HAMILTON* CREATOR

RIDE THE STREAM OF IDEAS: A DAILY MEDITATION

My dreams are so surreal, I don't think I could translate them into an actual piece of work, but my daydreams, when I sit on the couch with Lily and just drift in a relaxed, weightless cloud, are when the magic happens. My eyes might be closed, but usually I'm just staring with a soft focus on some random thing. In this half-awake, half-asleep state of zoning out, ideas rush in. Not all of them are worth remembering when I return to full consciousness, but it doesn't matter because I'm not looking for lightning to strike. I'm just allowing thoughts to flow between my ears and listening for the *clunk* when one gets stuck in there.

I live for that creative moment.

To assess your imagination flow:

1. **Choose a time every day when you're drowsy but awake.** Good options: the twenty minutes between your alarm going off and when you have to get out of bed; an hour after lunch, aka siesta time; the half hour after you get in bed at night but before you fall asleep.
2. **Lie down, or sit in a relaxed position.** Be comfortable, but not too comfortable that you actually crash.
3. **Close your eyes.** Lightly. No strain, just relaxation.
4. **Allow your mind to drift wherever it wants to go.** Don't judge the thoughts or try to guide them. The point is to just float on the current of your imagination, not steer the ship.

5. **If something strikes you as worth remembering, record it.** Using a voice memo recording app is best, because if you have to write something down, you'll take yourself out of the flow.
6. **After twenty minutes, open your eyes.** If nothing worthwhile came up, don't worry about it! You can't expect to find diamond-studded ideas every single day. But if you make this a practice, you'll notice that ideas do arrive with impressive frequency.

"diving into the cool." In hindsight, I wonder if it was the weed or just a creative vortex time of my life. It was probably a combination of working with talented people who gave me TLC and enhancing my imagination with a little THC.

Unicorn comedian George Carlin once said that he would write sober and get high for "punch up time" while editing. Where I stand now, I see the good and the bad in it. It's a decision every Unicorn has to face on their own. It can make you creative, and it can make you stupid. I choose not to smoke anymore because it hinders my efficiency, speed, and clarity, and it burns your brain cells—which I find it does to most when it comes into the workspace. It's an individual thing. Explore at your own risk.

IN DREAMS

Let your subconscious give you ideas. All you have to do is remember your dreams. The idea for the movie *Inception* came to director Christopher Nolan in a dream. Salvador Dali's famous "melting clocks" painting *The Persistence of Memory* was inspired by a dream. He often described his work as "hand-painted dream photographs." Even the lyrics of the Beatles' classic "Yesterday" came to Paul McCartney in the last moments of sleep. He woke up and wrote them down before he could forget.

Jiro Ono, a ninety-two-year-old Japanese sushi chef, has a restaurant in Tokyo that seats only ten people at a time, with a six-month wait to get in the door and three Michelin stars, the highest accolade any restaurant can receive. What makes Jiro's sushi so spectacular? He's simply the best, and obsessed with his art. Apprentices at this restaurant train for ten years before they're allowed to make rice. This man is so laser-focused on his art, he thinks about it 24/7, literally. In the documentary *Jiro Dreams of Sushi* Jiro describes getting ideas for new dishes when he's asleep, hence the movie's title.

INSPIRED BY LIFE

One of my favorite filmmakers is Unicorn Tim Burton. He gave a revealing interview to the *New York Times* about drawing inspiration from his childhood: "I felt like an outcast. At the same time I felt quite normal. I think a lot of kids feel alone and slightly isolated and in their own world. I don't believe the feelings I had were unique. You can sit in a classroom and feel like no one understands you.

"I would imagine, if you talk to every single kid, most of them probably felt similarly," he continued. "But I felt very tortured as a teenager. That's where *Edward Scissorhands* came from. I was probably clinically depressed and didn't know it." Or he was a Unicorn in a World of Donkeys. Negative-into-positive alert:

using his vivid imagination, Burton transformed his feelings of isolation as a child into a haunting, heartbreaking, and beautiful film.

Burton's goal is to shatter suburban conformity. In another interview, he said, "In the atmosphere that I grew up in, yes, there was a subtext of normalcy. . . . It's weird. I don't know if it's specifically American, or American in the time I grew up, but there's a very strong sense of categorization and conformity. [There was] no passion for anything. Just a quiet, kind of floaty, kind of semi-oppressive blank palette that you're living in. Why do I like clowns so much? Why are they so powerful to children? Probably because they are dangerous. That kind of danger is really what it's all about. It's that kind of stuff that I think gets you through life. Those are the only things worth expressing, in some ways: danger and presenting subversive subject matter in a fun way."

Unicorn Sarah Silverman writes, "I like talking about things that are taboo, because it makes them not taboo anymore. I grew up in a house where there were no taboos, so it came originally from a pretty innocent place, where I was shocked at the things that shocked people. I think I'm a troublemaker inside, if someone says, 'Don't say that,' it's all I want to say. And also, something I learned in therapy . . . which is darkness can't exist in the light, and then that made me think of something that Mr. Rogers said, which is, 'If it's mentionable, it's manageable.'"

When I first read that quote, I had this picture in my head of Sarah Silverman wandering the streets, searching for rules she could bulldoze over. Art or comedy is often steeped in chaos; to break boundaries, you have to mess shit up. The Silverman strategy is to look at society's rulebook and think up ways to tear it apart.

What do Burton and Silverman have in common? The inspiration of subversion and danger. Making trouble is the language of inspiration to jolt people out of their blank-palette lives. Shifting the universe is not light work. To make an impact, you need a heavy foot, a stomp that rattles the world.

WHERE DOES INSPIRATION GO TO DIE?

YouTube.

I know there are exceptions, and real creativity can be found there. But I find in the dance world, YouTube is a real problem. Aspiring dancers and choreographers put up videos of their pieces, hoping to catch the attention of someone in a position to help or hire them, but in the end, their original ideas wind up getting stolen by the very people they're trying to impress. A Unicorn calls this "robbery." A Donkey calls it "paying homage" or "being inspired."

There is a huge difference between being inspired by someone else's work and outright stealing it. Like any artist, I'm a student of history. You need to know your stuff and take in all those gorgeous, amazing moments from the past. But your job as a creator is to turn those influences upside down and inside out and to layer them with your own special sauce before you could respectfully and proudly call any "inspired" work your own. Get inspired! Don't steal!

THE KEY

To be inspired and shift the universe:

Be insatiable. You are constantly on the hunt for ideas, and always aware that they can come from anywhere, while you're awake, and in the dream stage. Know that inspiration is only the first step. Having that brilliant idea is useless unless you turn it into something of value to yourself and others, and you can't do that without breaking a sweat. Once you find your inspiration, manifest it. And don't wait. Strike while the idea is hot.

TALENT IS CHEAPER
THAN TABLE SALT.
WHAT SEPARATES
THE TALENTED
INDIVIDUAL FROM
THE SUCCESSFUL
ONE IS A LOT OF
HARD WORK.

STEPHEN KING, FIRESTARTER

DONKEYS PULL. UNICORNS *PUSH.*

BY NOW, YOU'VE AMASSED TOOLS FOR STANDING tall in your uniqueness, grounding yourself in authenticity, and, paradoxically, allowing your mind to float into the clouds. The next step on your journey is about harnessing all your powers to get shit done.

This is the Bust Your Ass chapter, Unicorns.

Success is in your hands, but only if you get them dirty.

I don't care if you're writing a novel or knitting a sweater, put in your best effort with focus, determination, and endurance. Be willing to reach the point of exhaustion or frustration, when you'd rather do *anything* other than work, but put your head down and work harder anyway. You can't rely on anyone else to push you. You have to do it yourself.

DO. THE. WORK.

Every morning, when I rise, the Devil says, "Oh shit, she's up."

That's what I tell myself anyway. Every day is another opportunity to conquer the world and to manifest whatever you want. As soon as you put your feet on the floor—or maybe not until after that first cup of coffee—make life your bitch. Your mantra is "Let's *do* this!" spoken with irony *and* intention. Optimal is your reward for effort and pain, and it is so worth it.

Donkeys wait for lightning to strike.

Unicorns get out the blowtorch and set fires.

DONKEYS WAIT FOR LIGHTNING TO STRIKE.

UNICORNS GET OUT THE BLOWTORCH AND SET FIRES.

I've pushed myself, and I've pushed the people I work with, hard. My reputation is that I'm a demanding, no-nonsense visionary, and I don't shy away from that one bit. To paraphrase Unicorn Joan Jett, "I don't give a damn about my reputation." My goal in choreography is to force the dancers to feel more passionate about their artistry, which will make my choreography shine and take them to a higher level of their craft than they have ever known.

Lazy Unicorns and Donkeys don't seem to care about being great, at least not as much as I do. In fact, they resent me for pushing them. People have asked me with all sincerity, "Can't you just care a little *less?*" Why should I care less about something I believe in and feel passionate about? It makes no sense. The coasters might slack and shrug, but I'm always shooting for full-strength Unicorn power. If you happen to take a class with me, or are cast in one of my shows, be warned: if you're not sweating, bleeding, crying, or your life isn't being changed in some way, you're not working hard enough.

My dad made my sister and me teach dance classes at our studio to pay for our Catholic school uniforms and teach us about responsibility. He wanted to instill in us a strong ethic at an early age and the idea that we had to work for what we had. He preached that to become an artist you have to go hard. If you're not ready to do battle for every piece, you might as well not create at all.

I have taught at a lot of dance conventions for kids, and I find it appalling that everyone wins. Back in the days when I competed, there were first-, second-, and third-place winners. If you lost, you went home and worked harder to improve for the next time. Losing made me hungrier to be better, insatiable. It made me my own harshest critic and inspired me to push myself to exhaustion. No one can do that for you. In a way, it's a hindrance to be naturally gifted as an artist. An easy win makes you complacent. As a boss, I'd rather hire good dancers who work their asses off and fight to improve than brilliant, lazy nightmares any day.

THE GODDESS OF ENERGY

If you ever need a role model for hard work, total commitment, and limitless energy, look no further than Unicorn Kristin Chenoweth. Right now, glance at her IMDb page. She's starred in movies, TV shows, and Broadway shows and makes albums. What I respect about her isn't merely the quantity of work she has done but the exceptional quality of it. She steals every scene she's in on pure personality and energy alone. Plus, she's gorgeous. Plus, she's gifted.

I've met Kristin once or twice and just fell in love with her humor, fun vibes, and fearlessness. She's unapologetically ebullient and doesn't have a fake bone in her body. To me, she's the living embodiment of the saying "There is no such thing as small roles, only small actresses." She is a tiny person who makes every part tremendous. You just know she's having a blast at whatever she does.

BLAME GAME

"It's not my fault."

"I didn't understand what you wanted."

"I didn't have the right material/equipment/support I needed!"

Donkeys make excuses and construct boundaries. Each one is a brick in the wall they build between their dreams and their reality. There are no valid excuses. You have to *make* your life happen, or you won't have one.

I once hired a "swing"—a dancer who fills in for different parts depending on need—in the cast of a Broadway show who'd really impressed me in his audition. But that was the last time he made a real, concerted effort. I guess he thought, once he had the job, he could coast. (How little he knew me!)

Instead of acknowledging his laziness and stepping it up, he blamed other people for his poor performance, saying, "The dance captains didn't give me the right information," and so on. We had several other swings in the show who wouldn't dare blame someone else if they sucked on stage. I gave this dancer ample opportu-

ONCE YOU DECIDE ON YOUR
OCCUPATION, YOU MUST IMMERSE
YOURSELF IN YOUR WORK.
YOU HAVE TO FALL IN LOVE
WITH YOUR WORK. NEVER
COMPLAIN ABOUT YOUR JOB.
YOU MUST DEDICATE YOUR LIFE
TO MASTERING YOUR SKILL.
THAT'S THE SECRET OF SUCCESS
AND IS THE KEY TO BEING
REGARDED HONORABLY.

 JIRO ONO, SUSHI ARTIST

nity to improve, but he seemed determined to be mediocre. I even once overheard him complaining about having to do the same routines every night. What did he expect? That we'd rechoreograph a Broadway show daily for his amusement?

Making excuses will not win you the love and loyalty of any boss, teacher, friend, or colleague—even if the dog really did eat your homework. Either do something well and right, or not at all. Even if you're in a low-level entry job, you have to give every ounce of your being, or you'll get stuck there. Climbing the ladder is a privilege, not a guarantee. Be the person who does more, and your work will get noticed, I promise. Get in the habit of being optimal at every moment of your life. I think there's a belief out there that you don't have to kick ass at a job you hate. Let me tell you: if you hate your job, do the work of finding another one, or bust your ass to get promoted out of it. Kick butt at every opportunity to create more of them. Slack off at every opportunity, and doors will slam in your face.

LIFE IS NOT A DRESS REHEARSAL

You might blow an opportunity, despite hard work. It happens to everyone, including me. How you handle defeat is another opportunity to succeed. It bothers me when people make a long list of reasons and excuses about *why* things go wrong.

If you get knocked down, fucking pick yourself up. It might take some time to recover, but it's a faster process if you see failure as an opportunity to learn how to do better next time, and not as an excuse to give up. You have no choice but to brush yourself off, take a deep breath, and keep going. Life isn't a dress rehearsal.

HOW TO GET IT DONE

Over the years I've picked up strategies to motivate me to do the work:

1. **Bit-by-bit.** The creative process is going from nothing to something. Although the big idea might pop into your head whole, you can only realize it piecemeal. One note at a time. One ingredient at a time. One page at a time. One movement at a time. So, break down your project into bite-size morsels, and make time for just a mouthful per day. Schedule creative blocks in your calendar, and don't make excuses or blow them off. Small bites add up to a feast.

2. **Alphabetically.** The ABCs of accomplishment: Always. Be. Creating. Procrastination is a problem for Unicorns because we're so easily distracted by shiny, sparkly new books, boyfriends, shows, crafts, arts. You could lose a whole day falling down an Internet rabbit hole. To ward off procrastination, set your phone to alert you at the top of every hour. Are you creating? No? Then shut down the Wi-Fi, and redirect your focus.

3. **Bossily.** One day, you might be the boss. If you were your own employee, would you be happy with your efforts, or would you fire your lazy ass? Flip a switch in your consciousness to become your own Amanda Priestly and demand your own best effort. Make yourself proud. Work hard enough to give yourself a promotion.

You can't go back in time, say the same lines over again (this time, with *feeling*!), or correct past screw-ups. But you do have the privilege of moving forward and living fully in the present and the future. Every day you're alive is a chance to go bigger, harder, and happier.

THE RULE OF THREE

Every day, do three things that will take you closer to your dreams. It might be writing three pages of your novel or sending three emails to people who might hire you. It might be walking three thousand steps if you want to firm up or practicing the piano for three hours. It could be any combination of these things: one hour at the piano, one networking email, one interview. The point is to actively pursue your goals and to count your progress. If you do three things every day, you'll have done twenty-one in a week, ninety in a month, over a thousand in a year. Each micro-accomplishment nudges your Unicorn Meter in the right direction.

When I was twenty, I doubted my talent and was trying as hard as I could to elevate my confidence. One of the three things I did to raise myself up every day was to reach out to people I admired, or anyone who might be in a position to lift my career. I sent a letter to a legend and one of the most respected choreographers of our time, Twyla Tharp, and asked her, "How do I make a dance?" My question must have sounded naive to her. I wasn't even sure why I asked it in the first place because I'd already been making movement and dances for a while, but I wrote the letter, sent it, and, incredibly, Twyla wrote back. I framed her letter and it's been hanging in my office for the last thirty years. Here's what she wrote:

Dear Mia,

Thank you for your recent correspondence. My best advice is:

1. *Seek your own counsel. If you know clearly what you think, you will know how to process the advice of others.*
2. *Spend your time on the making of your art, not your career. Career follows the work.*
3. *Always be your own most demanding critic.*
4. *Insist everything you do be a progression from your last work.*
5. *Try to learn as much as possible about the larger context of your work.*
6. *Do not be intimidated by history.*
I hope this will be of some service.
All the best,
Twyla

She was speaking Unicorn about finding the fire within, not comparing yourself to others or your own past, and stoking your curiosity. I read this letter often to remind myself of the principles of motivating myself to greatness. You can take this list and make it your own. You can frame the table of contents of this book to remind you of the twelve steps. You can make your own list of commandments or tenets that speak to you. But have a code of conduct to guide your life, and then use it to motivate you to get things *done.* Amazing things.

PUT ON YOUR RED SHADES:
A MOTIVATIONAL EXERCISE

Some days, I don't feel like being Superwoman, because I'm human, but I know that power is still in me to activate at any moment. I tell myself, "It's just a feeling. It exists, but it's temporary. You can shift it at your will." The power of the mind is incredible. You can use it to paint your attitude whatever color you want. When I feel tired and worn out, I play a mental trick on myself and put on a pair of invisible Red Shades, the ones that infuse me with energy. Or I put on my invisible tiara and stand a little taller. Or I slip on my imaginary spike-covered leather jacket to feel tougher.

Try this experiment next time you hear yourself making excuses or letting a bad mood or laziness stop you from reaching your day's goals. Say, for example, your goal is to write three pages of a novel, but you can't seem to get motivated.

1. **Sit down** in front of your computer. For a lot of people, the hardest part of writing is getting their ass in the chair (or getting into a sports bra to go to the gym, or onto the piano bench to compose a song). Just get your body in the physical position or in the right clothes.

2. **Put on your pair of imaginary Red Shades**. Imagine that the world is tinted red, the color of energy and power. It will get your blood going and fill you with energy. Concentrate on the infusion. What does it feel like? Like a jolt or a rolling river?

3. **Live the change**. Let the energy infusion carry you in its wake; open up your file, put your fingers on the keyboard, and start

typing, first a word, then a sentence, then a paragraph. Before you know it, you'll have three pages and possibly many more.

4. **Make it a practice.** Whenever you sit down, put on those Red Shades as part of the ritual of writing. As soon they go on, you mean business!

PREPARATION VERSUS IMPROVISATION

So you're all fired up, you've got on your Red Shades and are champing at the bit to get shit *done*. Fantastic! But . . . now what? How do you make the most of your motivation?

There are two schools of thought about creating. Some, like Unicorn portrait photographer Annie Leibovitz, think 90 percent of productivity is in the preparation. You've seen her iconic magazine covers for *Vanity Fair* over the years. I've been amazed how she captures the essential nature of her subject every time. Apparently, her photographs are the end product, the half-second click, at the conclusion of months of preparation. When she agrees to do a cover or a commission, she spends months researching her subject, every moment of their lives, their work, their personal life, how they've aged, what their goals are. In this period of getting to know her subject, she comes up with an idea of how to shoot this person in a way that illustrates who they really are. She next prepares the setting and styling she's envisioned so that, on the day of the shoot, all the work is done and there's nothing left but the final click.

On the other hand, some Unicorns rely on their gift of improvisation to reach their creative goals. Sometimes spontaneity is brilliant; sometimes it's a shit show. But the concept of winging it, of allowing yourself to be a vessel for creativity, is valid. Preparation can lead to prejudice and hinder the flow. When I choreographed Céline Dion's *A New Day*, I didn't do any research on Franco Dragone's style to prepare for working with him. I didn't want to be intimated by his work with Cirque du Soleil or run the risk of being influenced by his previous masterpieces. I wanted to go in with a fresh mind and eye.

When we first met, Dragone asked me, "Have you seen my work?" It was an awkward moment when I admitted I hadn't, but when I explained that I wanted to approach our project with no preconceived ideas, he understood. My coming in fresh benefited us both in the end, and we created a magnificent and magical show together.

Each artist has to decide which approach to use, and why. Really think it through. You might go back and forth between preparation and improvisation depending on the day and the job. That is the best balance for me.

When I choreographed the movie *Rock of Ages*, I dove deep into preparation. I had to create movements for a large cast that referenced the 1980s. I couldn't just show up on set and say to a dozen principal actors (including Catherine Zeta-Jones, Alec Baldwin, and Tom Cruise) that we would just wing it and see what happened. Before I arrived on the set, I researched each character, and each actor's dance abilities, and then created rough concepts for each piece. Preparation evolved into improvisation when the actors tried my movements on their bodies and added their own special sauce to my foundation. In collaboration, we came up with some brilliant moments. Layering turns a dry first pass into something nice and juicy. The more layers, the juicier it gets. For me, I expect to add six or seven layers of refining and punching up to my first "draft" before a piece is done.

TOM AND ME

Speaking of *Rock of Ages*, I had an incredible experience working with Tom Cruise. I thought I paid attention to detail, but Tom is relentless and a master at it. He enters a room like a ninja, and his energy is palpable.

In the movie, he plays Stacee Jaxx, an eighties rock god. When I brought him some ideas for the movement of his character, he'd already done extensive research and conceived of every detail of Stacee's life, style, and personality. Preparation is his artistry. Tom transformed into Stacee Jaxx in his body, movements, mannerisms, and awareness of how people reacted to him. He transformed into a rock star before my eyes. We worked together on every micromovement, how he'd dip one shoulder or open up his rib cage like a cowboy or roll in his pimp walk. His total commitment to becoming this character made me think of my artistry and use of detail. By creating the character and adding layers to his physical bearing, Tom was the consummate actor and his optimal self. He applies the same level of intensity to every role, in every movie. To me, Tom Cruise equals optimal.

THE KEY

To get the job done:

Don't make excuses. Even if you have legitimate complaints, put on your big Unicorn pants and find solutions instead of whining about problems. Fall in love with a work ethic to achieve your goals, so that effort feels good.

I BEGAN TO REALIZE HOW
IMPORTANT IT WAS TO
BE AN ENTHUSIAST IN LIFE.
IF YOU ARE INTERESTED IN
SOMETHING, NO MATTER WHAT
IT IS, GO AT IT FULL SPEED.
EMBRACE IT WITH BOTH ARMS.
HUG IT, LOVE IT, AND
ABOVE ALL, BECOME
PASSIONATE ABOUT IT.
LUKEWARM IS NO GOOD.

ROALD DAHL, DREAMER OF DREAMS

STEP TEN

EAT, PLAY, LAUGH

UNICORNS PUSH, PUSH, AND PUSH TO GET THINGS done, and our horns never glow more radiantly than when we are in a flow state of imagination and productivity.

But.

We also need to take a vacation from pushing. What I have found in the last year of putting "balance" at the top of my Unicorn agenda is that making room in my life for other things besides the hustle and grind actually improves my work. Ideas can't percolate into your consciousness if you're always busy thinking about what's next and doing things. Creativity depends on your doing absolutely nothing on occasion. Make mental space for the unexpected. It could happen while shopping, doing yoga, cultivating a garden, hiking a mountain, having a great meal with a close friend, or laughing.

You're a magical creature, so have some fun out there! Float like a butterfly and see where the wind takes you. Squeeze wonder out of every moment. Coax joy out of every day. You work hard, so allow yourself to rest and replenish. Think of this chapter as a little rest, the Sunday afternoon of the book, a window of time to savor and enjoy your many blessings. If you've had an intense workweek, be sure to spend your weekend eating and playing with your blaze, taking a stroll through the Rainbow Forest, or indulging in solitude.

Eat not only because you're hungry but also because food is *delicious*.

Play because it's the opposite of work, even if you love what you do. Balance!

Laugh because *everything* is funny if you look at it from a certain perspective.

All work and no play doesn't turn you into a Donkey, but it does slide your Unicorn Meter back toward the center of the continuum.

QUIZ: ARE WE HAVING FUN YET?

Put a check mark next to each activity if you've done it in the last seven days (only one check mark per, even for repeated instances):

1. Paid undivided attention to an animal. _____
2. Spent a continuous hour in nature without looking at your phone. _____
3. Played a sport or taken an exercise class that you enjoy (as opposed to one that feels like drudgery and torture). _____
4. Cooked a slow meal from scratch, and then ate it by yourself or with friends. _____
5. Got in bed with a good book. _____

6. Sat down with your journal or sketchbook and casually filled a few pages. _____
7. Laughed so hard you cried. _____
8. Zoned out for at least ten minutes. _____
9. Bonked to a satisfying finish. _____
10. Chilled or partied with beloved, trusted friends. _____

SCORING

1 to 3: Your life is out of balance. You really need to dial down your Unicorn drive and ramp up relaxation and fun a bit more each week. It might feel scary to take your hand off the switch, but when you return to work, you'll be more imaginative and productive—and (ask your colleagues) more cool to hang around with.

4 to 7: You're getting the bare minimum of soul replenishment each week. Try to throw in a few more opportunities for frivolity, rest, and laughter. Unicorns will always veer toward intensity, but downtime helps to refocus your mind. Staying loose prevents burnout.

8 to 10: Yay, fun-loving Unicorns! You have achieved balance between your active and restive selves. We all need to step back and enjoy the goodies of life (and I don't mean bling) so that we can go forward and achieve our larger goals.

THE REST IS HISTORY

After Lin-Manuel Miranda's Tony-winning musical *In the Heights* finally made it to Broadway, a process that took seven years, he had no idea what he was going to do next. Exhausted from years of work without a break, he took a vacation to Mexico and happened to pick up a big, fat biography to read by the pool.

"It's no accident that the best idea I've ever had in my life— perhaps maybe the best one I'll ever have in my life—came to me on vacation," Miranda once told interviewer Arianna Huffington. Of course, the biography he happened to read was Ron Chernow's *Hamilton.* "It was my first vacation from *In the Heights.* The moment my brain got a moment's rest, *Hamilton* walked into it."

The rest is history. Or, I could say, Miranda's rest reconceived American history and then made Broadway history. The musical *Hamilton* went on to win eleven Tony Awards, launched the career of every actor in the original cast, and made Lin-Manuel a household name. If he hadn't taken a break, it might never have happened.

MAKE YOUR OWN FUN

The idea of having fun might set off anxiety in some Unicorns if they think, "Who am I going to have fun with if I don't have any friends?"

Let me tell you, a popular person who's surrounded by friends might feel completely alone. A Unicorn can be alone and still burst with joy and happiness. You don't need friends to have a good time or to live to the fullest. You only need yourself. I often travel, go to shows, cook meals, drink a glass of wine by myself. I can book a week in the Bahamas after a grueling work cycle to reward and romance myself. I fly next week to a beachside suite for one! I might talk to the person on the barstool next to me, but I'm more likely not to and just to luxuriate in peace and quiet.

Being alone is a selfish pleasure. The fire within needs fuel, and

I fan the flames with silence. If you're always busy, surrounded by other people, and booked solid from morning until night, when do you figure out what you need for yourself? People who are flurries of activity and appointments make me wonder how comfortable they are with themselves, if they're afraid to slow down and look inward because they might not like what they see. If you take time to be alone and quiet and to look inward, truth will arrive. In meditation or prayer, whatever you want to call it, the next phase of your life will solidify in your mind. Without that clear picture of what you want to do, you can't manifest it.

I dream on Sunday, and manifest on Monday.

UNICORN'S ESCAPE

Shifting the planet and making magic take a toll, Unicorns. Hit the reset button in life by losing yourself in a passion or a hobby. Delight in the weird, the niche—the micro-niche—something strange that'll make a Donkey say, "What the *fuck* are you talking about?" Having an escape is not the same thing as questing for inspiration. Going to museums and screening movies are not hobbies. But picking through flea market tables for antique dolls and building birdhouses from toothpicks *are*. The difference is that learning is purposeful and escapes are just mind-sweeping fun.

Some Unicorns and their hobbies:

- Mark Twain designed his own suspenders.
- Nikola Tesla, inventor, adored pigeons and fed them every day at a park near his house.
- Frida Kahlo was an avid cactus and succulents gardener.
- Albert Einstein played the violin.

- Prince loved to play basketball and then make pancakes after games (yes, just like in the famous Dave Chappell skit; he once griddled cakes at midnight for me, too).
- Angelina Jolie collects daggers and samurai swords.
- Sarah Jessica Parker is into knitting.
- Nick Offerman of *Parks and Recreation* is a master wood-worker and actually sells handcrafted furniture at his crafts shop in Los Angeles.
- Filmmaker David Lynch roasts his own coffee.
- Emily Dickinson loved to bake bread.

A UNICORN'S FAVORITE FOOD

When the last dance class of the day ended at the Joe Michaels Dance Studio, Dad invited his older longtime students to stick around for dinner. He'd make a massive amount of spaghetti and meatballs to feed everyone. These spontaneous pasta feasts often happened late at night. I remember filling my bowl, inhaling the hot noodles and spicy sauce, and falling into bed in a carb coma.

Apart from the fact that eating carbs makes you fat, you need to strike a balance between eating healthy and eating whatever you want without guilt and with pleasure. Enjoy every bite of yummy food! Quaff wine! Even though I think he would have liked me to be thinner, my dad instilled in me a love of food and celebrating life. If you work so hard and don't take moments to play and enjoy *and indulge*, what's it all for?

SOMETIMES PEOPLE LET
THE SAME PROBLEM MAKE
THEM MISERABLE FOR YEARS
WHEN THEY COULD JUST SAY,
"SO WHAT." "MY MOTHER
DIDN'T LOVE ME." SO WHAT.
"I'M A SUCCESS BUT I'M
STILL ALONE." SO WHAT.
IT TOOK A LONG TIME FOR ME
TO LEARN IT, BUT ONCE YOU DO,
YOU NEVER FORGET.

ANDY WARHOL, POP ICON

SWEAT

When I'm focused on a job and have to work sixteen hours a day to reach my deadline, the first thing that gets cut from my schedule is exercise. I say, "I'll get back to it later when all this is behind me." But exercise is the one thing that should never be cut. I have learned from experience that sweating for just twenty minutes a day reduces work pressure and ass expansion by half. As a kid, you run and play every day. When we become adults, we forget the importance of that.

Lately, I've been rewarding myself daily (language is important! Speak of exercise as a gift you give yourself, wrapped up in a pretty bow) with boxing lessons, Soul Cycling, trampolining, and yoga classes. Not only does exercise boost my energy and turn me into a shapely Warrior Goddess but also it gets me out of my head. The running to-do list in my mind stops scrolling because, if I don't stay focused on what's happening in the ring, I might get a right hook to the jaw. During yoga, I fixate on my breath.

You don't have to take a class or join a gym to do mind-clearing, juicy exercise. You can break a sweat by going for a run or fast walk or by chasing your dog around the yard or dancing your ass off in your bedroom. Get your heart going, concentrate on your body, free your mind every day, and then come back to your Unicorn goals, energized and refreshed, with a tighter Unicorn ass.

LILY AND ME

My dog, Lily, is a Unicorn. We found each four years ago when I contacted a breeder in search of an English bulldog. I was hoping to find a miniature English bulldog, small enough to fit in a shoulder bag, but the breeder said she had only one puppy left, a female, who was so not little. She was *huge*, the largest puppy in that litter. She described the dog as "chunky" and "the opposite of dainty" but with a beautiful face. (Sound familiar?) I nearly fell out of my chair when the breeder explained why she hadn't sold her yet: "She has underdeveloped hind legs," she said. "I'm not sure they'll ever grow to normal size. She has some trouble walking and I don't think I can sell her."

Immediately, I started crying.

I still get teary-eyed just thinking about it.

This is my dog, I thought. We were meant for each other.

I brought her home on December 27, my Christmas gift to myself, a roly-poly ball of cuteness and slobber. Her big pink tongue permanently hangs out of her mouth, and she's got these big, beautiful, wet brown eyes that gaze at me with pure acceptance. Her legs eventually grew to be powerful and strong, just like her mommy's.

I could not love a human baby more than I love Lily. She is my home. Being with her makes it okay to do nothing but cuddle on the couch. We don't eat off the same plate, but we have the same taste in food (we both love it all).

When I spend a weekend with Lily, just the two of us hanging out, playing with her toys, taking walks, sitting across the table from each other at dinner, time slows down. It's just the two of us, and our dreams. I prefer her company to that of people a lot of the time, because humans expect conversation and reciprocity and there's pressure to deliver and perform. I often don't have the energy or will to be the person they want me to be. Lily helps me reconnect with myself. Her unconditional love supports my self-love. Being with her is intimate, precious time to sink into myself.

THE WANDER OF IT ALL: A WEEKLY ADVENTURE

The fastest and easiest way to play and soak up the wonder and beauty of the Rainbow Path is to put on a pair of decent sneakers or hiking boots and take a walk outside, in nature, for one hour just once a week, on a Sunday, perhaps, if you have weekends off. Go to a park, or a mountain trail, or the beach, and wander.

You have to leave your phone at home.

I'm not going to give you a lecture on phone use. I get it. We love and need our devices. But for one hour a week, you have to break out the crowbar and pry the phone out of your hands. The world will not fall apart in that time. The big job offer will not materialize then. Any news or text can wait. To increase your Unicorn powers, forget about your Facebook status for a little while.

A phone can be a shield that blocks you from magic. If you are clutching it like a lifeline and checking your notifications every three minutes, you won't notice the sparks, no matter where you are. So leave your phone at home, exit one reality and dive into the cool of another one.

1. **Drive, subway, taxi, or walk to the nearest expanse of pure nature.** If you live in a city, go to the biggest park. If you live near a lake or the ocean, or a mountain, whatever, make a beeline to the foot of the trail or the entrance to the beach.

2. **Commence exploration.** Look around at the trees, plants, clouds, mud, moss, dappled sunlight through the leaves, birds, and bugs. Talk to them all—including the plants. You are a carbon-based life-form, just like them. Get acquainted.

3. **Bathe in oxygen.** In Japan, "forest bathing" is a health practice and has been proven to lower blood pressure and stress. Imagine the clean air is breathable water that you are immersed in and wading through. Each breath clears away the toxic garbage of negative emotions and stress inside your body.

4. **Observe.** When you've hit the halfway point in your walk, sit down on a rock or the ground and be silent for a good five minutes. Allow yourself to listen to your body—your beating heart, your breath—and the natural world around you. The wind in the leaves, mysterious rustling or chirping. Look while listening. Maybe you'll notice that you are never alone in the woods. You share the forest with the bugs and birds, the sprites and fairies, the angels and God. Do they have any wisdom for you today? If you listen closely, you might hear it.

5. **Return to "reality."** Once you're back home, you might notice that you're not so keen to pick up that phone after the blissful hour away from it.

6. **Do it again.** Make a regular date with nature, at least once a week. It only takes an hour with the trees and bees to tune in to magic and reset your stress level, *or . . .*

(continued)

For those of you who can't get into nature or are in the mood for an urban wander, you can still escape one reality and dive into another. This time:

1. **Bring your phone, but power down first.** You might need directions to get home later, so have it as a tool, but don't look at it while wandering.
2. **Walk another way.** When you leave your front door, if you usually go right, today, go left. If you know a street well, be mindful to avoid it and walk down one you don't know. In a city as vibrant as New York, you can find whole new worlds on every block. Venture out.
3. **Pop in.** If you're walking down a new street, and you happen to come upon a place that strikes a curiosity chord, check it out! Always let instinct and curiosity be your guides while wandering, and in your professional and creative lives.
4. **Strike back.** If someone happens to strike up a conversation with you, respond. Introverts, don't worry. I'm not suggesting you make a new friend. If you are okay with it, make a three-second connection. Meeting or observing new people is part of the urban wander adventure.
5. **Follow the wind.** If you don't know which way to go next, let the wind point you in the right direction. Just float along, as if you were a butterfly, carried along by the breath of the universe.

SANCTUARY

Along with the joy of Lily, my apartment in Tribeca is full of magical objects, many of which I found or designed myself. I breathe in the charm of small things without irony, and let all of these interesting pieces inspire me. Quite literally, I live in my aesthetic. Just being at home is a happy respite from reality.

Your point of view as an artist is a part of who you are. How you live in your perspective, from the way you dress to how you do your hair, decorate your home, and cook your meals, is reflected back at you and represents you in the world. Every object and choice are extensions of you. How you live every moment (because you don't get them back) leaves an impression on you, and on others.

Many of my Unicorn friends have escapes that are related to collecting and design. I'm not saying you have to spend a fortune on clothes and furniture. However, an attention to detail in your surroundings and in your style as a person who moves through public and private spaces will be felt. What you see, hear, smell, taste, and touch, the sensory input of your life, informs your output as an artist. So have fun feathering your nest or building a cool wardrobe. If a garment doesn't make you feel like you, don't wear it—get rid of it! If something in your decor upsets you, throw it out or recycle it. Everything around you in your space needs to be Unicorn-worthy.

MAKING ROOM

If you don't have "room" for wonderful things (like a long restaurant meal, great sex, or belly laughs), you need a bigger "house." You are not your career. You are a sparkly, frisky creature that needs to jump, trot, and play, so clear some space for your health, sanity, and relationships. It's fine to prioritize your creative goals, but if they take up so much room that everything else is crowded out, you become a one-track, one-trick, boring Unicorn. I believe you can have it all, even if you put creative first (as I do), as long as you stay aware of balance and open up that mental space for other things.

Recently, I learned this lesson myself when I finished a demanding job that consumed all of my time and attention for nearly a year. I fell into the void and landed on my feet, but it was a long time before the dust settled and I could assess where I was. I realized that all I had was another line on my résumé, some money in the bank; I was fat, unhealthy, and lonely but "successful." I took a good, hard look around, saw that the landscape was sparse. I had my career, which fills and sustains, but not much else. I thought, *How do I change my life?* The answer became a mantra: "Make room."

Make room for fitness.

Make room for happy relationships.

Make room for rest.

Make room for me.

I had to trash some garbage from my life, getting rid of material and human clutter, things and people who took up space but didn't do much for me. It was a literal cleaning out of junk from my apartment and a metaphorical sweeping away of toxic thoughts, relationships, and bad habits. I made room for myself, and now I feel light and free, and ready to wander.

THE KEY

To make room for rest and restoration (this is an easy one):
Eat. Play. Laugh. Love. Create.

DO NOT COMPROMISE YOURSELF. YOU'RE ALL YOU'VE GOT.

 JANIS JOPLIN, RULE BREAKER

STEP ELEVEN

PLAY NICE IN THE SANDBOX

OKAY, SUNDAY IS OVER. IT'S MONDAY MORNING again, and Unicorns have to go to work and deal with other people, most of whom are basic and don't "get" them. It's not impossible to thrive in a Donkey-majority school or workplace. You just have to manage others and yourself.

In our work culture, you most likely have to work on a team or collaborate. As a choreographer, I have to bond with dancers and translate everything through their bodies. I work intimately with a mix of Donkey and Unicorn performers and producers to fulfill my purpose and make my art. I've learned about collaboration, listening to others, being open to every possibility. It can be extremely frustrating to deal with "groupthink" and to compromise—many Unicorns find compromise a challenge, to put it mildly—but I believe that every experience has value, even when you want to tear your hair out. In one job or assignment, you might learn your craft. In another, you might learn how to manage people. It's all to your benefit, and every new thing you figure out about yourself is a nudge of the meter in the right direction. Embrace the challenge.

WHAT THE FUCK?

Never conform. Define yourself. The world worships the original.

And yet, Unicorns still have to live and function in a Donkey's world. As much as they appreciate us for our innovation, they do look at us like we're "other." And we are! For one thing, we've got this huge fucking iridescent, glowing horn on our forehead. It can't be ignored, and it will always make Donkeys shake their heads and say, "What the fuck?"

I love that. I love mystifying people and making jaws drop. Unicorns have the power to shock and amaze. When you walk into a room with your glitter, you'll bewilder. You'll make them squirm in their seats. I heard a great story about Unicorn actor Joel Grey. He was such a rule breaker, such a force of nature, that when he went into auditions, he would go off script, jump all over the room, explore the character so relentlessly that producers would brace themselves as soon as they saw him. They didn't know what he was going to do, but it was always magic. He *wowed* every time he showed up, and he became a legend.

In the professional realm, expect to be questioned about pretty much everything you do. You will always have to prove yourself, especially if you are a woman. Even now, women are expected to be twice as smart, funny, talented, accomplished, and brave as any man to reach the same level of power and success. Women in creative fields have to be the biggest, baddest Unicorns around—and, even then, you'll have to pee rainbows and shit gold to be taken seriously and respected. If a man does what you do, he's a genius. If you do it, you'll be questioned. Just my two cents.

Bring it. Put on those Red Shades and welcome the challenge like it's a long-lost friend. It took me twenty years to learn to push back and say, "Really? You doubt me? You don't believe in me? Just watch this."

"Just watch" and "Just listen" are the only appropriate answers to "What the fuck?" Success is the greatest revenge on the nonbelievers.

I revel in my "watch me" moments. I can't wait to be challenged so I can prove them all wrong. Once the people in your way understand and know your power, when it's obvious what you can bring to the world, the doubting Donkeys will back down. What I like to see when I walk into a room is people saying, "Oh, shit, she's here. What's she going to do?" The look of bewilderment mixed with fear feels to me like a compliment, like respect.

Don't make doubting Donkeys fear you because you're "mean" or "a bitch." They'll fear you because you're brilliant. They don't know how far you're going to rock their world today.

A SEASON IN CORPORATE HELL

I'll tell you right off that my tolerance for corporate culture is very low. I've worked for a big corporation with entrenched "traditions" about how "things are done," and it was torture. Like scooping out my brain through my mouth. I *hated* it—but I busted my ass as hard as ever and was proud of the work I did there. When it was all over, though, I realized that my bosses didn't particularly want me to break new pavement. They couldn't have cared less if my work was original and important.

If all I'd done was roll out a review of my greatest hits, conform, and stay safe, they would have been just as happy as if I'd reinvented the wheel.

Big corporations do not care about your Unicornness. In fact, their employee handbook might as well be called *How to Be a Donkey*. Whatever advice I have to offer, Brand X will recommend the opposite.

QUIZ: ARE YOU A CORPORATE DRONE?

Answer **T or F** to the following questions:

1. Are you comfortable with having zero freedom of expression? **T or F**
2. Are you okay abiding by a dress code? **T or F**
3. Does producing mediocre work, over and over again, seem appealing? **T or F**
4. Are you more concerned with playing it safe than taking risks? **T or F**
5. Do you consider passion about your work to be a negative? **T or F**
6. Will you happily adapt to the corporate culture, regardless of what it is? **T or F**
7. Do you see yourself as a cog in the machine? **T or F**

SCORING

If you answered T to any of these questions, I have to wonder why you're reading this book. Unicorns chafe at conformity, limits, and rules, anything that puts them and their ideas in a steel trap.

THERE'S A POINT . . .

WHEN YOU HAVE TO

CHOOSE WHETHER TO BE

LIKE EVERYBODY ELSE

THE REST OF YOUR LIFE,

OR TO MAKE A VIRTUE

OF YOUR PECULIARITIES.

URSULA K. LE GUIN, CREATOR OF NEW WORLDS

I understand that sometimes, in every Unicorn's life, a corporate job is the only option, and you have to suck it up and work for the Man to pay the rent. I have been there (which explains why I have an insider view on this kind of place). I walked away from my stint in corporate hell with a reputation for being "difficult" and "too passionate." I can't work any other way, so, at the end of my contract, I did leave and took with me much experience and growth and a better idea of what to do and what not to do next time.

While you are working at Brand X, do not drink the poison! Ramp up your Unicorn quotient during off-hours; keep dreaming, writing your book on the side, looking for a creative job, and reinforcing your horn in every other aspect of your life. Keep working toward being the ultimate expression of your uniqueness so that, when opportunity knocks and that steel trap opens, you are ready to make your escape.

UNICORNS ARE POLITICAL ANIMALS

Unicorns need to be political animals: diplomatic, flexible, and shrewd. Part of the work of creating is managing your feelings of the people around you—and your own. Some tips about collaborations and the things I have learned along the way:

1. **Always start from a position of humility**. Even if you know beyond a shadow of a doubt that you're better/right/more deserving, you still have to be diplomatic and navigate through other people's pride. As long as you come off as humble—respectful and deferential—you won't be seen as a threat to anyone in the room.

2. **Instead of fighting over details, flood them with options.** When someone doesn't like a gesture or a piece of my work, I don't pout or complain or tell them they're wrong. I turn around and come up with fifteen new options to choose from. This way, they have to make a decision and it's always going to be something I like.

3. **Use limits to force yourself to be more creative.** Janis Joplin said, "Don't compromise yourself," and I'm in complete agreement with the Hippie Goddess about integrity. However, as I've gotten older, I've learned that limits aren't actually restrictive. Compromising with other people is a test of your creativity. Sailing a craft through a narrow passage requires greater skill than having the whole ocean to maneuver in. Sometimes greatness lies in slim spaces. Imposed limitations give you the freedom to explore what's possible.

4. **Dazzle.** Always remember that someone is paying you actual money to do a job. The person who signs the checks holds a measure of control over what you do and when you do it. You might be smarter, more talented, more brilliant than your boss. But until yours is the name on the front of the check, you have to earn your fee and show the boss that you take the job seriously, even if you know it's not your ultimate destiny.

5. **Sometimes you play nice in the sandbox by putting down your shovel and going home.** There's bending, and then there's shriveling. If I'm working with a Donkey who insists on holding me back, I might respectfully walk away. Toxic people do more than squander your creativity; they snuff it out. No job is worth that. Speaking of which . . .

CLASH OF THE UNICORNS

Many times, I've scaled a steep learning curve! Well, that is part of a creative life, existing in a constant state of realizing how much you have to learn. And I have learned so much about the joy and misery of working with others.

It's hard to collaborate, whether you're working with Donkeys or Unicorns. I've worked with geniuses like Céline Dion and Prince, and loved every second of it. I've worked with appreciative Donkeys who have said, "I know enough to step back and let you do what you do," which brought out the best in me. And then, there were disastrous collaborations with Unicorns who scared the crap out of me—and not in an "uncomfy is fierce" way.

Around the turn of the century, I worked with an iconic pop diva to choreograph her world concert tour. "Total fucking nightmare" was her workplace persona, but a more generous description would be "hard to please." I took dealing with her reputation as a personal challenge. I was determined to make her love my work. It was my first big job as a choreographer, and I had a lot at stake, so you can imagine my anxiety when, right off the bat, the diva and I clashed horns. She just didn't like me.

At our every meeting, she would burst into the studio and rake me over the coals. I took to wearing a scarf because each time we were in the same room, I broke out in hives. An assistant told me that the diva hated my makeup and my hair—I was in my white dreadlocks stage. This surprised me because the diva never seemed to look at me. Respectful people make eye contact, no matter how much they hate your hair. It was awful being around her.

I'm not a quitter, so I kept trying to please her and, in the end, I kept giving her options and working creatively with her notes without flinching (in her face). I managed to do some good creative work, despite her setting off all the insecurities I'd worked hard to defeat. When I remember her now, I think of a quote from Madeleine Albright: "There is a special place in hell for women who don't support each other."

Thanks to that experience, I learned to speak up on my own behalf, not to be intimidated into silence, and to run from anyone who poisons creativity. Another line on your résumé or a few more dollars in the bank are not worth feeling unhappy or existing in a toxic environment.

UNICORN-DONKEY WORKPLACE MATRIX

You'd think having a Unicorn for a boss or colleague would be ideal. The two of you could brainstorm together, and every day would be like trotting down the Rainbow Path in tandem, casting flower petals in the wind. It doesn't always work like that, unfortunately, but it can! Check out the positives and negatives of working with Unicorns and Donkeys in the matrix on the following page.

BOUNCING BACK

Say, you get fired.

It happens.

What sets the winners and losers apart is how they react after a blow. Generally speaking, Extreme Unicorns—which you are, having been through eleven steps already—are the dreamers of dreams. You prefer to float along on a pixie dust cloud. The harsh

	BOSS OR COLLEAGUE	BOSS OR COLLEAGUE
Your workplace persona is a	• You know exactly what everyone wants and expects. • You don't feel pressure to push yourself or impress anyone. • If you do push yourself, even a little bit, you will shine. • You feel like you're just a cog in the machine. • Your workplace is like a holding pen. You do what you need to do and then you go home.	• A Unicorn boss will push you to go beyond your expectations of what you can do. • When you get praise from a Unicorn, it's like touching a rainbow. • The Unicorn in the office will expect creativity from you, and that will intimidate or inspire you. Probably both. • Their directions might not be clear, which will be frustrating.
Your workplace persona is a	• You stand out and are considered a reliable idea creator. • If you're a political animal, you can bring out the Unicorn in other people and make a better workplace environment for everyone. • On the other hand, you might be seen as odd and aren't invited to happy hours with the Donkeys. • Stubborn Donkeys will fight your original ideas. • Your colleagues and boss might be intimidated by or envious of you.	• Best case: You inspire each other to reach magical heights. • On the way there, you might disagree and have to go to your separate corners to regroup. • Too many ideas can be a bad thing: if you both have your heads in the clouds, you might float away in different directions. • In some cases, your horn clashes are fatal. You won't be able to work together and live.

realities of the world can come as a shock. Although you might like to trot down the Rainbow Path in the glorious sunshine for all eternity, there will be storms. In life, no one, neither Donkey nor Unicorn, gets out unscathed and unscarred. You need resilience, integrity, and a solid core of inner strength to survive the down-pours.

THE GIFT OF FAILURE

In 2008, J. K. Rowling delivered an inspiring commencement address about resilience to Harvard grads. I'd like to share an excerpt of it here:

> Why do I talk about the benefits of failure? Simply because failure [means] a stripping away of the inessential. I stopped pretending to myself that I was anything other than what I was, and began to direct all my energy into finishing the only work that mattered to me. Had I really succeeded at anything else, I might never have found the determination to succeed in the one arena I believed I truly belonged. I was set free, because my greatest fear had been realized, and I was still alive, and I still had a daughter whom I adored, and I had an old typewriter and a big idea. And so rock bottom became the solid foundation on which I rebuilt my life. You might never fail on the scale I did, but some failure in life is inevitable . . . unless you live so cautiously that you might as well not have lived at all—in which case, you fail by default.
>
> Failure gave me an inner security that I had never attained by passing examinations. Failure taught me things about myself that I could have learned no other way. I discovered that I had a strong will, and more discipline than I had suspected; I also found out that I had friends whose value was truly above

the price of rubies. The knowledge that you have emerged wiser and stronger from setbacks means that you are, ever after, secure in your ability to survive. You will never truly know yourself, or the strength of your relationships, until both have been tested by adversity. Such knowledge is a true gift, for all that it is painfully won, and it has been worth more than any qualification I ever earned.

FAILURE: THE MYTH

My attitude about failure is slightly different from J. K.'s. I don't think failure even exists. If you worked hard and learned while you were creating a project, a relationship, a vision of yourself, you didn't fail. Things might not have worked out the way you hoped, but as long as you truly did your best and didn't let Donkey ego and fear hold you back, a so-called failure is still a success because you grew stronger. If you figured out that you suck at something you have two choices: aim yourself in a new direction, or work harder and be better at what you've chosen.

Instead of beating yourself up for finding yourself in the same bad situation (job, partner, financial mess) again and again, ease up on the pressure to change. Forgive yourself and grant yourself time to heal and recover. It's entirely possible that the larger lesson you need to learn is to relax, breathe, and accept that you, a magical Unicorn with a shimmering hide and glowing horn, are also human. Next time you feel crushed under the pressure to "be better next time," meditate on self-love instead.

- In all likelihood, you will make the same mistake again until you learn not to repeat it.
- It might take an entire lifetime to break out of some behavioral

loops, but because Unicorns strive to evolve until the very end, you have that to look forward to.

- Worrying about fixing yourself as soon as possible will probably prolong the process and block you from gaining the insight you need.

- It's not possible to find meaning in every experience *as it happens.* Instead, focus on being the authentic, humble, powerful, compassionate, hardworking, bouncy, risk-taking Unicorn you are, and have faith that growth is happening, whether you feel it or not.

- Believe me, meaning will come in good time. You will learn what you need to learn, but not on demand. Personal evolution is sort of like a cat. If you chase it, it'll run away and hide under the bed. But if you are patient and calm, it will come to you, sit on your lap, and shed. Or something like that.

BETRAYED!

I've faced some extraordinary betrayals in my career, events that were hard to bounce back from. People have lied to me, stolen from me, and stabbed me in the back. Unicorns can be sensitive, trusting, and a bit naive, unsuspecting of the ruthlessness of others. But there's an old saying that rings true for me: "You're stronger where you're broken."

Sometimes it's hard to find *anything* positive in a miserable experience. Once, when I was broke and in desperate need of a job, my best friend and assistant at the time went behind my back and shared my work with the choreographer of a new show. The choreographer was, shall we say, "inspired" by it, and the show was a huge hit. Both my (former) best friend and the choreographer became fantastically wealthy from this project. Unfortunately, choreography isn't protected the way a song or a book is copyrighted, and there was absolutely nothing I could do about it.

The theft went way beyond my friend being inspired by my work. She gave the choreographer step-by-step breakdowns of my company repertoire. If you saw my company perform and this show side by side, you wouldn't be able to tell the dance moves apart. The worst part was that I felt betrayed by my best friend. I've worked hard for everything I have and wouldn't dream of stealing another person's art, especially that of someone I had shared special moments with and spent years in the studio setting working on her body.

How to turn this train wreck into a limousine? I bounced back by reminding myself that steps can be stolen, but talent can't. The success of the show was proof that audiences responded to my work, even if they didn't know it was mine. I said to myself, "It's my old stuff, they can have it. There's a lot more where that came from." The experience spurred me to come up with something new and innovative. Ever since, when I'm creating a new piece and need to access fury, I think about that experience and ex-friend.

My mantra for bouncing back after a betrayal: "Hope for the best and forgive the worst in others." You got stabbed in the back? Dwelling on it is a self-inflicted wound. I don't forgive for the sake of those who wronged me. I do it to stay clean on the inside. Anger and bitterness pile up like garbage inside you, which is called disease. You have to get that shit *out*, or I believe it will literally kill you. Make sense of it and why people do what they do. And most of all, forgive for you.

THE KEY

To work well with others and keep your integrity:

Ride along. My father used to say, "When life goes up, enjoy it. When it goes down, don't worry. It'll go back up. Make good out of the bad. Make the best out of the good. Live the hell out of every day." That's what I've aspired to do. I haven't always succeeded, but when I get frustrated about something that doesn't work out, I thank God for the experience and look forward to the roller coaster's next trip back up to the top. It's not about the high-highs or the low-lows but about how we manage the rising and the falling. Do so with a sense of humor and the faith that every day brings you closer to your dreams.

NO ARTIST IS AHEAD OF HIS TIME. HE IS HIS TIME, IT'S JUST THAT OTHERS ARE BEHIND THE TIMES.

 MARTHA GRAHAM, MOTHER OF MODERN MOVEMENT

STEP TWELVE

IT'S ONLY JUST BEGINNING

THE UNICORN'S JOURNEY HAS TWELVE STEPS. Each one counts, and each one builds on the last, so that you get stronger and weirder as you progress on the Rainbow Path. By now, your horn is the envy of every magical creature out there. You are more confident in what you can do, more humble in your worldview, and more optimistic about the future. It's all about learning, and so far, you've aced:

Step One: Respect. It's no small thing to be born a legend. You took on the responsibility to wear your horn like it's a crown of jewels.

Step Two: Authenticity. With your shields lowered, you looked inward and searched your heart and soul for truth, and really got to know who you are.

Step Three: Courage. Once you accepted yourself, you accepted that not everyone else has loved, is in love, or will love you for your uniqueness. Different is intimidating to lesser minds. Just knowing that helped you find the silver lining in the darkest of clouds.

Step Four: Toughness. With self-awareness and humility, you grew a thick hide to deal with the kind of criticisms that used to crush you.

Step Five: Connection. Your new confidence attracted people to you, and you found your blaze when you wanted company and learned to enjoy solitude just as much.

Step Six: Fear. With a solid foundation in humility and authenticity, and the support of trusted friends, you put the previous steps to work on pushing past fear to the uncomfortable edge where all creativity happens.

Step Seven: Faith. It takes faith to jump into the unknown, and you found something to believe in—God, magic, and miracles, and yourself.

Step Eight: Inspiration. After running and leaping into the unknown, you restocked the creative cupboards with curiosity and learning.

Step Nine: Motivation. You turned all that inspiration into something meaningful by putting your head down and doing the work, with determination and discipline.

Step Ten: Restoration. As motivated as you are, you took time to rest and relax, to let your mind and body recharge for what's to come.

Step Eleven: Cooperation. You have to live in the world with people who don't necessarily get you, so you adapted and stretched to cooperate with integrity and without compromise— and put springs in your hooves to bounce back well in case things didn't go as planned.

Next, the final step, the one you'll be doing for the rest of your life: **evolution**.

Unicorns never stop seeking, growing, and evolving, which is why your greatest years and work always lie ahead. You have reached the most magical place of all—a state of mind where your past makes sense, your present is a gift you unwrap daily, and the future is boundless.

There can be no room for doubt in a Unicorn's belief system, including the faith that the best is yet to come. This goes beyond simple optimism. It's the certainty in your core that you aren't done yet, that you have more to give, even after you've already given so much.

I'd like to spend a few pages sharing with you how I've evolved in the last year, while working on this book about Unicorns—a book about you, and a humbling, terrifying, exhilarating adventure for me. It only confirms my belief that no matter how well you know yourself, you've still got so much more to learn.

THE RAINBOW PATH HAS NO END

You've worked hard and learned so much, and it all brought you here, to the place where you are ready to shift the universe. Say, you do. Say, you break new pavement and the world adores you. What then?

Warning: Creativity is an eternal uphill climb. The exceptional never rest on their laurels. The voice that whispers in my ear "What next?" is a push from the universe to make sure I keep driving and evolving.

I feel obliged to reach higher because I'm never satisfied by what I've created so far. I've never fully loved anything that I've done. I might like it a lot, but I think I've fallen short of brilliance and I'm very much in the hunt for that.

Now, some might say that it's a tragedy never to be satisfied, to feel like you haven't reached your full power, even after decades of striving.

I say, "Thank God!"

You can't count on anyone to hand you a dollar, an idea, a job, an Emmy. I believe that the universe won't let the exceptional have it easy because Unicorns are at their most brilliant when they are hungry. I kind of wish creativity wasn't always like pushing a boulder up a mountain. Sometimes, I wish I could just float from one great thing to the next, but that is not my life, or perhaps anyone else's, either.

Truman Capote, a Super Unicorn, was fascinated by the danger of getting what you think you want, and he started a novel about it called *Answered Prayers*. As he said, "More tears were shed over answered prayers than unanswered ones." When you are old enough to look back at your life, you'll see, as I do, that every job you prayed for and didn't get opened the door for another job that was important for your artistic and personal growth. I was crushed at the time I got the bad phone call, but before too long, I was thrilled about the way things played out. I've learned not to get upset and to just keep pushing, to keep going for optimal, and setting myself up for the next big thing that's meant for me. I trust destiny. I trust God. I trust the universe. I trust myself.

SEE THE FUTURE

This year, I'm doing my first vision board. It's full of photos and notes of everything I want for myself as I evolve. Here's what's on mine, as inspiration for yours:

THE WORST THING
YOU CAN DO WITH
THIS WORK WOULD
BE TO TICK OFF
ALL THE BOXES:
"I DID THAT,
I DID THAT AND
I DID THAT."

WILLIAM FORSYTHE, LEGENDARY CHOREOGRAPHER

- Accepting my beautiful body as it is rather than changing to fit into someone else's ideal
- A beautiful home by the water
- This book
- Love
- Lifelong friends
- Nonstop laughter

Anything that gives me butterflies goes up on the board, and I'm not ashamed to want and crave things, material and spiritual, for myself. My evolution is to allow myself to desire things, to give myself permission, after decades of struggle, to be greedy. I'm learning for the first time in my life to want what I want, no apologies.

LISTEN TO THE NOW

The evolved Unicorn's favorite word is *allow*. I'm allowing trust. Allowing things to happen the way they're supposed to. Allowing myself not to stress out about not being in control.

I've been hustling since I was eight years old, and in my business, I rarely if ever took the time to listen. I had this masculine energy that said, "Go, go, go!" All of a sudden, I'm in a feminine space of receiving and listening, for the first time, to what my body, mind, and spirit are telling me I need.

"What do I need?" is the opposite of "What do I want to achieve?"

What do *you* need? How often do you even ask?

My answer lately is to live in the luxury of loving myself without limits, by sweating and eating well, getting rest, and connecting with people I adore. I feel myself softening and getting clearer.

I've fought for everything I wanted in the past, and now, suddenly, the rebel warrior side of me wants to shed her armor. I'm evolving into softness and balance. I understand who I am as a woman, artist, and businessperson. I visualize myself stepping into the most glorious time of my life.

I desperately want that for you, too.

Celebrate yourself every step of the way.

Write a love letter to yourself every day.

Why *not?*

Whatever is beautiful and happy in your life *is* your life.

MORNING MEETINGS WITH MYSELF

I used to wake up and think about "goals." But now I've softened and my morning meetings with myself are about setting intentions. The point isn't to stress myself out and add to the list of shit I have to do but to remind myself why I'm here and to ask, if this were my last day on Earth, how would I want to live it?

Usually, my intentions are reminders to treat myself and other people well. To think about how I can take my career one step further, or how I can take my relationships one step closer to being as close and loving as possible. This book is about nudging you closer, one inch at a time, to the ultimate expression of who you are. I've been setting the intention to do that, every day, with my first breaths. Maybe by the time I'm ninety, I'll get there and be as cool as the man I consider to be a Grand Daddy Unicorn of all time. . . .

THE UNICORN PALACE

Ninety-year-old Tony Bennett recently gave an interview about aging. "The whole secret for anyone my age is to keep learning, keep growing, keep creating," he said. "It's the opposite for many people, when they turn eighty-nine or ninety years old, they feel, 'Well, I've done it all, so I better just relax.' I think that's a failure. As long as you're alive, keep learning and be curious."

Tony the Great paints every day, keeps recording, and collaborates with young Unicorns like his bestie Lady Gaga, who he adorably calls "Lady." He gives back by doing benefit concerts all over the world. He loves his wife, eats well, and has the life goal of making people happy and promoting peace on Earth—a Unicorn to the core.

As we know by now, it is not a Unicorn's destiny to have it easy. A Unicorn goes through life being misunderstood and the underdog and the oddball. But the question you must ask yourself is, "Do I want to live the extraordinary life of a Unicorn, or do I want to live the easy basic life of a Donkey?"

A reward awaits you toward the end if you choose the Rainbow Path. When you're a younger Unicorn, you have a lot to prove and are constantly pushing and pushing to make a name for yourself, make a difference, be heard, and be the standout you know you are. There comes a point, as we mature and reflect on all the things we've done in our lives as Unicorns and whether we've been loved or hated, when we reach a sense of joy, relief, and acceptance, when we can exhale and say we've truly lived and celebrated every step along the way.

Instead of worrying about being a legend for the rest of the world, I'm working on being a legend to myself. The blessing and reward come when you can simply live in your Unicorn Palace as the ultimate version of who you are. When you are happy with yourself and the choices you've made, you've "made it."

When you painted the picture of your life, what colors and textures did you use? Were they beige and pastel, or colorful, wild, fun, fearless, and unapologetic? Are you worried about what other people think, or have you fully evolved to say, "I don't give a fuck what anyone thinks or says about my journey"?

I've been called difficult. I've been called a bitch. I've lost friends, money, love, and gained weight along the way. Ultimately, nothing matters except how you feel about yourself and your journey of love, friendship, and laughter. There's just you and your Unicorn life. Celebrate and bask in it.

THE FINAL KEY

One final message for you newfound Extreme Unicorns: You've got all you need to succeed, so keep on trotting along the Rainbow Path.

Never say, "My work here is done." Every day is another opportunity to dream, create magic, make a life, make art, meet someone, and learn to fly.

My wish for all of you is to live without regret and to laugh your ass off every single day.

And my fairy-tale ending is to live a fabulously full, delicious life and to continue making a difference until my last breath, when I say, "Wasn't that fun?" and die happy.

ACKNOWLEDGMENTS

This book would not be possible without these incredible people: Val Frankel, Laura Mazer, Sharon Kunz, Kerry Rubenstein, Frank Weimann, and Steve Troha. Thank you all for believing in this project and making it possible to share with the world. And thank you to all the Donkeys and Unicorns I have encountered along my Rainbow Path: The ones who broke my heart and the ones who lifted me up and inspired me, the ones who misunderstood my passion and the ones who celebrated it. You shaped who I am, and I am grateful to all of you. I share this book with you.

ABOUT THE AUTHOR

MIA MICHAELS is devoted to touching people's lives with passion and emotional expression. She is best known for her Emmy Award–winning appearances on *So You Think You Can Dance* and for her creation of the choreography for Broadway's *Finding Neverland.* She has also choreographed Vegas stage shows and world concert tours for artists such as Céline Dion, Madonna, Prince, and the Rockettes. She lives in New York City with her English bulldog.

I AM

I AM THAT I AM THAT I AM

AND I THANK GOD I AM!

 MIA MICHAELS